The Passover Haggadah

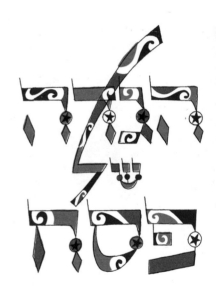

Compiled and Edited by
RABBI MORRIS SILVERMAN

REVISED AND EXPANDED EDITION
*with a modern translation, explanatory notes,
historical background, and new readings*

Designed and Illustrated by
EZEKIEL SCHLOSS

THE PRAYER BOOK PRESS

Media Judaica, Inc. • Bridgeport, Connecticut

To ALTHEA

My אשת חיל

פיה פתחה בחכמה
ותורת חסד על לשונה
משלי לא

She opens her mouth with wisdom;
On her tongue is the teaching of kindness.

Proverbs 31:26

Revisions and Expanded Material
Edited by JONATHAN D. LEVINE

1975 Printing

This edition of the Haggadah includes the *complete* traditional text, in Hebrew and English, as well as numerous comments, explanations, and contemporary readings which have been placed at various points in the Service.

Among the contemporary readings are:

A Prayer for Russian Jewry	page IV
The Message of Passover	page 2
Remembering the Holocaust	page 45
In Gratitude for Israel	page 66
Proclaim Liberty for All	page 82

TRANSLITERATION

To encourage participation, several Hebrew passages which are often chanted in unison appear in transliteration *within* the text, in addition to the transliteration of Passover Songs on page 84.

COMPANION RECORDING

The musical portions of this Haggadah have been recorded by the Media Judaica Chorus under the title "Sounds of the Seder" (cassette and 33-1/3 rpm record) and may be obtained from the publisher.

Leader lifts a special matzah, sets it aside, and says:

THE MATZAH OF HOPE

This matzah, which we set aside as a symbol of hope for the three and a half million Jews of the Soviet Union, reminds us of the precious links which unite us with them.

As we observe this festival of freedom, we know that Soviet Jews are not free.

> They are not free to learn of their Jewish past or to hand it down to their children.

They are not free to learn the languages of their fathers.

> They are not free to express their Jewish identity.

They are not free to teach their children to be community leaders, teachers, or rabbis for future generations. Nor can they obtain Jewish books.

> As their voices have risen in Jewish pride and protest, we add our voices to theirs.

And we shall be joined by all people of good will who are aroused by the wrongs inflicted on Soviet Jews.

> Thus shall our brethren know that they have not been forgotten. They shall yet emerge into the light of freedom.

iv

PREFACE TO THE REVISED EDITION

It has been conservatively estimated that there are more than two thousand variant editions of the Passover Haggadah. Why, then, another Haggadah? How does this Haggadah differ from others?

This Haggadah is both traditional and modern. It is designed for the family at home, for the public Seder, for study groups, and for Passover institutes. It includes concise instructions for the various ceremonies as well as comments and historical explanations which present the ancient traditions in modern form. Supplementary material has been interpolated in the text with a view to stressing the contemporary significance of the Seder.

The traditional Haggadah is a unique document of Jewish history, literature, legend, folklore, and song. Some of its words and rituals are ancient, linked to religious observances in Jerusalem more than two thousand years ago. Some selections were added in the eighth and ninth centuries; others were incorporated as late as the fifteenth century.

This edition of the Haggadah has been brought "up to date" with comments by contemporary scholars, and readings pertaining to the annihilation of the six million Jews in the Holocaust, and to the modern rebirth of the State of Israel.

We have preserved the classical text of the Haggadah in its entirety. The concept of *K'lal Yisrael*, the universal Jewish People, is given vivid expression when Jews everywhere use the traditional Haggadah, hallowed by use through the centuries—reinterpreting anew those passages which may seem obscure or dated at a particular time and place.

In this edition, we have arranged the Hebrew and English texts in a format which encourages both group reading and individual recitation.

It is our hope that this Haggadah will help "to turn the hearts of parents to their children and the hearts of children to their parents." May both old and young share the spirit of the Seder, and reaffirm its ancient message that all men have the God-given right to be free.

PREPARATION FOR THE SEDER

Preparation for the Seder begins weeks in advance. Some of us have nostalgic memories of mother preparing for Passover, of the thorough housecleaning which culminated in the colorful ceremony of father and children symbolically removing, by candlelight, the crumbs of bread; the excitement of taking out the Passover dishes; and the joy associated with purchasing new garments for the Passover holiday.

While some share these fond memories, others may now be seeking, for the first time, the warmth and spirituality associated with the Passover holiday.

Just as one cannot fully enjoy an opera without knowing something of its historical background, its musical motifs, and the roles of the leading characters, so one cannot appreciate the Seder without knowing the Haggadah's themes and development, its procedures and rituals.

THE LEADER

The Leader should review the text *in advance,* and be prepared to recite several basic portions of the Haggadah, lead the singing of the Passover melodies, *explain* and coordinate the service.

The Leader should also select some of the explanatory notes to be read or discussed, and should assign several passages for recitation by individuals.

THE SEDER TABLE

The Seder table should be attractively set. Spring flowers are appropriate. (Passover is also called *Ḥag Ha-Aviv*—the Festival of Spring.) Candlesticks, Kiddush cups, Passover tray, matzah cover or tier, pitchers of water and decanters of wine are essential to the Seder table.

At the head of the table there should be placed a "Ceremonial Plate," the Leader's Kiddush cup, a decanter of wine, a bowl of salt water, and three matzot placed one on top of the other in a matzah cover, or in a wooden or silver matzah tier. A large wine cup for Elijah should be placed in the center of the table.

There are a number of opinions as to the arrangement of the items on the Seder plate. The following is recommended:

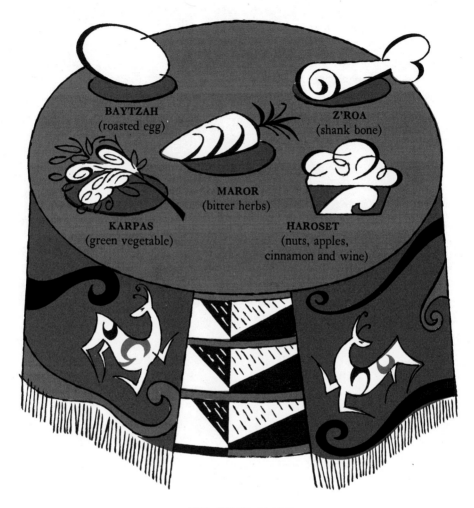

BAYTZAH
(roasted egg)

Z'ROA
(shank bone)

MAROR
(bitter herbs)

KARPAS
(green vegetable)

HAROSET
(nuts, apples,
cinnamon and wine)

THE SEDER PLATE

The Ceremonial Seder Plate should contain the following: (1) a charred shank bone of lamb (*Z'roa*); (2) a roasted egg (*Baytzah*); (3) bitter herbs (*Maror*), *i.e.* horseradish; (4) some greens, such as parsley, celery or lettuce (*Karpas*); (5) a mixture of grated nuts, grated apples, cinnamon, and wine (*Haroset*). (*Optional:* A strip of cinnamon bark may be placed near the *Haroset*, further symbolizing the bricks without straw which our forefathers were forced to make in Egypt.)

To accelerate the distribution of the ceremonial matzah, parsley, bitter herbs, etc. (especially when there are many guests present), *duplicate* "ceremonial plates" may be placed around the table. One or two guests may assist in distributing the *Karpas, Matzah, Maror,* etc. If possible, each person at the table should be provided with a Kiddush cup, a small dish of salt water, and a small dish of *Maror* and *Ḥaroset*.

Sufficient wine should be provided so that each participant may partake of four cups. If many guests are present, several decanters should be conveniently placed so as to expedite the filling of the four cups.

(While some adhere to the custom of having a large pitcher of water at the table for the washing of hands, others use several small water containers and basins, such as *Mayim Aḥaronim* receptacles.)

SIGHT AND SOUND

The decoration of the Seder table and of the household can be a meaningful family project *before* the Seder—and will add to the festival spirit *during* the Seder.

Traditionally the host or the Leader wears a white robe known as a *Kittel*. The white robe is a reminder of the vestment worn on sacred occasions by the priests in the ancient Temple. White is a symbol of festivity, gladness, and freedom and is thus appropriately worn during the Seder when we hope for the final deliverance from bondage and misery. The host, garbed in white, is sure to fascinate the children, and the impressiveness of the *Kittel* will long linger in memory. (Women may design such a robe for their husbands.)

On the left side of the host's armchair, two pillows are placed—for "leaning" while reciting certain parts of the service. (For the explanation of this custom, see page 10.)

Music is a vital part of the Seder service. Heinrich Heine wrote: "Even those Jews who have fallen away from the faith of their fathers . . . are moved to the very depths of their being when they, by chance, again hear the old Passover melodies once so dear to them."

Wherever possible Hebrew passages should be *chanted* rather than merely read. "Sounds of the Seder," a companion recording for this Haggadah, is available from The Prayer Book Press. Music for the Seder is found in such standard works as *The Songs We Sing*, compiled by Harry Coopersmith.

Passages to be recited in English and Hebrew should be outlined in advance so that all guests and members of the family may participate.

MATZAH AND ḤAMETZ

When the Israelites hastily left Egypt, they had no time to bake ordinary bread with leaven (*Ḥametz*). For this reason, as a commemoration, unleavened bread (*Matzah*) is used on Passover. In accordance with the command "There shall be no leaven seen in your home" (Ex. 13:7), the Jewish home is cleansed of all *Ḥametz* before Passover; thus, "spring housecleaning" has become part of the Passover tradition.

ORDER OF THE SERVICE

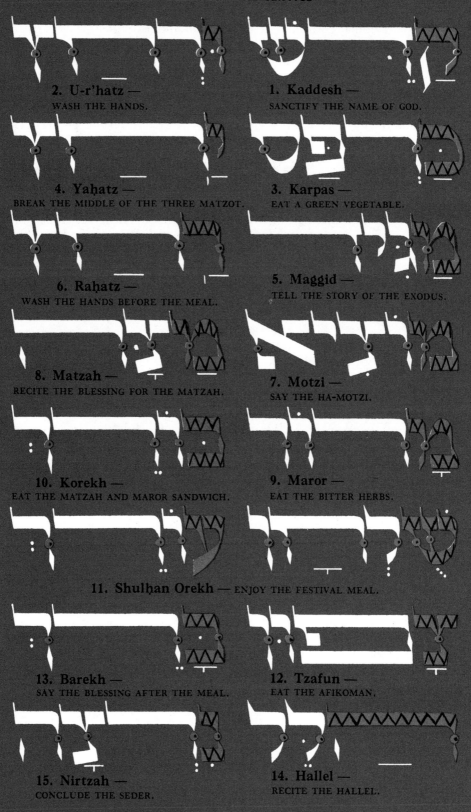

2. U-r'hatz —
WASH THE HANDS.

1. Kaddesh —
SANCTIFY THE NAME OF GOD.

4. Yaḥatz —
BREAK THE MIDDLE OF THE THREE MATZOT.

3. Karpas —
EAT A GREEN VEGETABLE.

6. Raḥatz —
WASH THE HANDS BEFORE THE MEAL.

5. Maggid —
TELL THE STORY OF THE EXODUS.

8. Matzah —
RECITE THE BLESSING FOR THE MATZAH.

7. Motzi —
SAY THE HA-MOTZI.

10. Korekh —
EAT THE MATZAH AND MAROR SANDWICH.

9. Maror —
EAT THE BITTER HERBS.

11. Shulḥan Orekh — ENJOY THE FESTIVAL MEAL.

13. Barekh —
SAY THE BLESSING AFTER THE MEAL.

12. Tzafun —
EAT THE AFIKOMAN.

15. Nirtzah —
CONCLUDE THE SEDER.

14. Hallel —
RECITE THE HALLEL.

CEREMONY OF REMOVING ḤAMETZ

The ceremonial cleansing of the home should be meticulously carried out, along with the ancient and colorful ceremony of searching for and removing leaven (*Bedikat Ḥametz* and *Biur Ḥametz*). By candlelight—a child may carry the candle—parents and children go from room to room, "searching" for leaven. With a large feather and wooden spoon or bowl, the father collects crumbs of bread (previously placed where they may be easily found). Both the crumbs and receptacle are wrapped together and burned the following morning (see p. xi).

This ceremony can be a particularly thrilling, dramatic experience for children and is another link with the Jewish tradition.

Our Sages regarded leaven as a symbol of *Yetzer Hara*—the "evil inclination." They likened our evil desires to the leaven in the dough of life. By removing the leaven from our homes, we symbolize our desire for liberation from the corrupting influences which make us subservient to our passions and evil desires. (This interpretation illustrates the interdependence of ritual and ethics in Judaism.)

THE HAGGADAH

The name of the Seder text, "The Haggadah," is related to the word *V'higgad'ta* (Ex. 13:8) *"and you shall tell* your son" (the story of the Exodus). *Haggadah* means "telling." We *tell* the story of the deliverance from Egyptian bondage. The Haggadah was originally brief.* Succeeding generations have added interpretations, legends, and songs.

A visit to a Jewish museum affords the rewarding opportunity to view Haggadahs in many lanaguages and from all parts of the world, artistically illuminated and illustrated. Some of these, produced before the age of printing, and reverently written by hand, were the medium through which great artistic talent was expressed.

WORSHIP, STUDY, AND CELEBRATION

The Seder is a religious observance—an occasion for praising God as the source of all life and liberty. In Judaism, God is worshiped not through prayer alone, but also through *study*. The Haggadah affords a rich opportunity for such an experience. Our Sages said: "If three persons have eaten together and have not discussed Torah, it is as though they had eaten of the sacrifices to the dead. . . . But if three persons have eaten together and have spoken words of Torah, it is as though they had eaten from God's own table" (Pirkei Avot 3:4). This thought is particularly relevant to the Seder meal, at which we are supposed to reflect upon the ideal of freedom and the continuity of Jewish history.

*Pesaḥim, ch. 10.

The ritual of Passover night is known as the *Seder*—a Hebrew word which means *order:* the "order of procedure" or "agenda of the service." This agenda consists of fifteen different items, some brief, others longer. The meal itself is one of the items—and is usually the longest. Fifteen distinctive phrases summarize these fifteen items in the "Order of the Seder program" (see p. ix). In many homes a folk melody for this Order of the Service (*Kaddesh U-r'ḥatz*) serves as a prelude to the formal start of the Seder.

On the evening before the night of the first Seder (on Thursday night when the first day of Passover occurs on Sunday), the search for leaven begins with the following blessing:

Praised be Thou, O Lord our God, King of the universe, who hast sanctified us with Thy commandments and enjoined upon us the mitzvah of removing leaven before Passover.

בָּרוּךְ אַתָּה, יְיָ אֱלֹהֵינוּ, מֶלֶךְ הָעוֹלָם, אֲשֶׁר קִדְּשָׁנוּ בְּמִצְוֹתָיו, וְצִוָּנוּ עַל בִּעוּר חָמֵץ.

After the search is completed and the leaven and receptacle are wrapped together, the following declaration is made:

May all leaven in my possession which I have not seen or removed, be regarded as non-existent and considered as mere dust of the earth.

כָּל חֲמִירָא וַחֲמִיעָא דְּאִכָּא בִרְשׁוּתִי, דְּלָא חֲמִתֵּהּ וּדְלָא בְעַרְתֵּהּ, וּדְלָא יְדַעְנָא לֵהּ, לִבָּטֵל וְלֶהֱוֵי הֶפְקֵר כְּעַפְרָא דְאַרְעָא.

The following morning after breakfast (on Friday morning when the first day of Passover falls on Sunday), the leaven is burned, and the following final declaration is made:

May all leaven in my possession, whether I have seen it or not, or whether I have removed it or not, be regarded as non-existent and considered as mere dust of the earth.

כָּל חֲמִירָא וַחֲמִיעָא דְּאִכָּא בִרְשׁוּתִי, דַּחֲזִתֵּהּ וּדְלָא חֲזִיתֵּהּ, דַּחֲמִתֵּהּ וּדְלָא חֲמִתֵּהּ, דְּבַעַרְתֵּהּ וּדְלָא בְעַרְתֵּהּ, לִבָּטֵל וְלֶהֱוֵי הֶפְקֵר כְּעַפְרָא דְאַרְעָא.

הַדְלָקַת נֵר שֶׁל יוֹם טוֹב

BLESSING OF THE FESTIVAL CANDLES

Before sunset and prior to sitting down for the Seder, the mother and daughters light the candles and pray:

Our God and God of our fathers, may the rays of these festival candles cast their glow upon the earth and bring the radiance of Thy divine light to all who still dwell in darkness and in bondage. May this season marking the deliverance of our ancestors from Pharaoh, arouse us against any despot who keeps man bowed in servitude. In gratitude for the freedom which is ours, may we strive to bring about the liberation of all mankind. Bless our home and our dear ones with the light of Thy spirit. Amen.

On Sabbath add words in brackets.

Praised be Thou, O Lord our God, King of the universe, who hast sanctified us with Thy commandments, and enjoined upon us the mitzvah of kindling the [Sabbath and the] Festival lights.

בָּרוּךְ אַתָּה, יְיָ אֱלֹהֵינוּ, מֶלֶךְ הָעוֹלָם, אֲשֶׁר קִדְּשָׁנוּ בְּמִצְוֹתָיו וְצִוָּנוּ לְהַדְלִיק נֵר שֶׁל [שַׁבָּת וְשֶׁל] יוֹם טוֹב.

Praised be Thou, O Lord our God, King of the universe, who hast kept us in life and sustained us, and enabled us to reach this season.

בָּרוּךְ אַתָּה, יְיָ אֱלֹהֵינוּ, מֶלֶךְ הָעוֹלָם, שֶׁהֶחֱיָנוּ וְקִיְּמָנוּ וְהִגִּיעָנוּ לַזְּמַן הַזֶּה.

Parental Blessing

For sons:

May God bless you as He blessed Ephraim and Manasseh.

יְשִׂמְךָ אֱלֹהִים כְּאֶפְרַיִם וְכִמְנַשֶּׁה.

For daughters:

May God bless you as He blessed Sarah, Rebecca, Rachel and Leah.

יְשִׂמֵךְ אֱלֹהִים כְּשָׂרָה, רִבְקָה, רָחֵל וְלֵאָה.

Conclude with the following threefold blessing:

May God bless you and keep you;

יְבָרֶכְךָ יְיָ וְיִשְׁמְרֶךָ.

May God cause His spirit to shine upon you and be gracious unto you;

יָאֵר יְיָ פָּנָיו אֵלֶיךָ וִיחֻנֶּךָּ.

May God turn His spirit unto you and grant you peace.

יִשָּׂא יְיָ פָּנָיו אֵלֶיךָ וְיָשֵׂם לְךָ שָׁלוֹם.

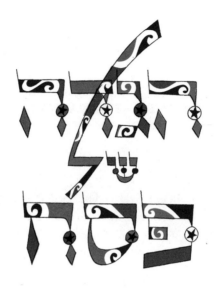

THE HAGGADAH

THE MESSAGE OF PASSOVER

Leader or Responsive Reading

elcome to our Seder! Tonight we observe a most ancient, colorful, and significant festival. The Seder takes us back to those events which occurred more than three thousand years ago. We recall the Egyptian bondage of the Children of Israel and their deliverance by God.

History tells us that many other peoples were also enslaved by tyrants. But the Israelites were the first to rebel against serfdom, and to institute a holiday dedicated to freedom. Most nations observe an Independence Day, but the observance of the birthday of Jewish freedom is unique because of its profoundly religious character. Every Jewish home becomes a sanctuary, every table an altar where gratitude is expressed to God, the Author of liberty. Through prayer and song, ritual and symbol, custom and ceremony, we look upon ourselves as though *we* were among those enslaved and then brought forth unto freedom.

This self-identification with the past of our people, helps us better to appreciate the freedom that is ours, and more fully to understand the plight of such of our brethren as still dwell under the shadow of tyrants. The Seder calls upon us to do all in our power to emancipate them from tyranny.

The Seder, which keeps alive in us the love of liberty, has a significance also for all mankind. Freedom which is one of man's most precious gifts, must not be taken for granted. In every age it must be won anew. The Pharaoh of the Exodus is symbolic of the tyrants of our day as well as of the tyrants in every era of history.

If a people is anywhere exploited and oppressed, then nowhere is man really secure. Freedom is indivisible. The Seder expresses the need of man's eternal vigilance in the struggle to preserve and advance the cause of freedom and human dignity. May God grant that freedom become the lot of all the children of men.

1. Kaddesh — Sanctify the name of God —

Fill the first cup of wine.

Leader

We begin this service by sanctifying the name of God and proclaiming the holiness of this Festival. With a blessing over wine, the Jew ushers in the Sabbath and all Festivals. As we lift the cup of wine, symbol of joy, let us now welcome the Festival of Passover.

In unison

Our God and God of our fathers, we thank Thee that Thou hast enabled us to gather in happy fellowship, again to observe the Festival of Freedom. Just as for many centuries the Seder has brought together families and friends to retell the events which led to our freedom, so may we this night be at one with Jews everywhere who perform this ancient ritual linking us with our historic past. As we relive each event in our people's ancient struggle, and celebrate their emergence from slavery to freedom, we pray that all of us may keep alive in our heart the love of liberty. May we dedicate our lives to the abolition of all forms of tyranny and injustice.

As we partake of this cup of wine, symbol of joy, we acknowledge Thee our Creator, our Father, our Liberator. We praise Thy holy name in the traditional words of the Kiddush:

On Sabbath add:

And there was evening and there was morning — the sixth day. Now the heavens and the earth — yea, the whole universe — were finished. And by the seventh day God had finished the work which He had made; and on the seventh day He ceased from all the work which He had made. Then God blessed the seventh day and hallowed it, for on it He rested from all the work which, in creating, He had made. (Gen. 1:31–2:3)

וַיְהִי עֶרֶב וַיְהִי בֹקֶר

יוֹם הַשִּׁשִּׁי. וַיְכֻלּוּ הַשָּׁמַיִם וְהָאָרֶץ וְכָל צְבָאָם. וַיְכַל אֱלֹהִים בַּיּוֹם הַשְּׁבִיעִי מְלַאכְתּוֹ אֲשֶׁר עָשָׂה, וַיִּשְׁבֹּת בַּיּוֹם הַשְּׁבִיעִי מִכָּל מְלַאכְתּוֹ אֲשֶׁר עָשָׂה. וַיְבָרֶךְ אֱלֹהִים אֶת יוֹם הַשְּׁבִיעִי וַיְקַדֵּשׁ אֹתוֹ, כִּי בוֹ שָׁבַת מִכָּל מְלַאכְתּוֹ אֲשֶׁר בָּרָא אֱלֹהִים לַעֲשׂוֹת.

בָּרוּךְ אַתָּה יְיָ אֱלֹהֵינוּ מֶלֶךְ הָעוֹלָם בּוֹרֵא פְּרִי הַגָּפֶן׃

Baruḥ atta Adonai, elohenu meleḥ ha-olam, boray p'ri ha-gafen.

Praised be Thou, O Lord our God, King of the Universe, Creator of the Fruit of the Vine.

Praised be Thou, O Lord our God, King of the universe, who didst choose us from among all people for Thy service, and exalted us by teaching us holiness through Thy commandments. Out of love hast Thou given us, O Lord our God, [Sabbaths for rest,] holidays for gladness, festivals and seasons for rejoicing, among them [this Sabbath day and] this day of the Feast of Unleavened Bread, the season of our freedom, a festival of holy assembly, commemorating our liberation from Egypt. From among all peoples hast Thou chosen us, and didst sanctify us by giving us Thy holy [Sabbath and] Festivals as a joyous heritage. Praised be Thou, O Lord, who hallowest [the Sabbath,] Israel and the Festivals.

בָּרוּךְ אַתָּה, יְיָ אֱלֹהֵינוּ, מֶלֶךְ הָעוֹלָם, אֲשֶׁר בָּחַר בָּנוּ מִכָּל עָם, וְרוֹמְמָנוּ מִכָּל לָשׁוֹן, וְקִדְּשָׁנוּ בְּמִצְוֹתָיו. וַתִּתֶּן לָנוּ, יְיָ אֱלֹהֵינוּ, בְּאַהֲבָה [שַׁבָּתוֹת לִמְנוּחָה וּ]מוֹעֲדִים לְשִׂמְחָה, חַגִּים וּזְמַנִּים לְשָׂשׂוֹן, אֶת יוֹם [הַשַּׁבָּת הַזֶּה, וְאֶת יוֹם] חַג הַמַּצּוֹת הַזֶּה, זְמַן חֵרוּתֵנוּ, [בְּאַהֲבָה] מִקְרָא קֹדֶשׁ, זֵכֶר לִיצִיאַת מִצְרָיִם. כִּי בָנוּ בָחַרְתָּ, וְאוֹתָנוּ קִדַּשְׁתָּ מִכָּל הָעַמִּים, [וְשַׁבָּת] וּמוֹעֲדֵי קָדְשֶׁךָ [בְּאַהֲבָה וּבְרָצוֹן] בְּשִׂמְחָה וּבְשָׂשׂוֹן הִנְחַלְתָּנוּ. בָּרוּךְ אַתָּה, יְיָ, מְקַדֵּשׁ [הַשַּׁבָּת וְ]יִשְׂרָאֵל וְהַזְּמַנִּים.

On Saturday night continue with HAVDALAH.

On other nights continue with SHE-HE-ḤE-YA-NU.

Havdalah

Praised be Thou, O Lord our God, King of the universe, Creator of the light of fire.

Praised be Thou, O Lord our God, King of the universe, who makest a distinction between the sacred and the secular, between light and darkness, between Israel and the heathen, between the seventh day of rest and the six days of work. Thou hast made a distinction between the higher sanctity of the Sabbath and the lesser sanctity of the Festival, and hast hallowed the Sabbath above the six days of work. Thus hast Thou distinguished and sanctified Israel with Thine own sanctity. Praised be Thou, O Lord, who distinguishest between the sanctity of the Sabbath and the sanctity of the Festivals.

בָּרוּךְ אַתָּה, יְיָ אֱלֹהֵינוּ, מֶלֶךְ הָעוֹלָם, בּוֹרֵא מְאוֹרֵי הָאֵשׁ.

בָּרוּךְ אַתָּה, יְיָ אֱלֹהֵינוּ, מֶלֶךְ הָעוֹלָם, הַמַּבְדִּיל בֵּין קֹדֶשׁ לְחֹל, בֵּין אוֹר לְחֹשֶׁךְ, בֵּין יִשְׂרָאֵל לָעַמִּים, בֵּין יוֹם הַשְּׁבִיעִי לְשֵׁשֶׁת יְמֵי הַמַּעֲשֶׂה. בֵּין קְדֻשַּׁת שַׁבָּת לִקְדֻשַּׁת יוֹם טוֹב הִבְדַּלְתָּ, וְאֶת יוֹם הַשְּׁבִיעִי מִשֵּׁשֶׁת יְמֵי הַמַּעֲשֶׂה קִדַּשְׁתָּ; הִבְדַּלְתָּ וְקִדַּשְׁתָּ אֶת עַמְּךָ יִשְׂרָאֵל בִּקְדֻשָּׁתֶךָ. בָּרוּךְ אַתָּה, יְיָ, הַמַּבְדִּיל בֵּין קֹדֶשׁ לְקֹדֶשׁ.

4

She-he-ḥe-ya-nu

בָּרוּךְ אַתָּה, יְיָ אֱלֹהֵינוּ, מֶלֶךְ הָעוֹלָם, שֶׁהֶחֱיָנוּ וְקִיְּמָנוּ וְהִגִּיעָנוּ לַזְּמַן הַזֶּה.

Baruḥ atta Adonai, elohenu meleḥ ha-olam, she-he-ḥe-yanu, ve-kiy'manu, ve-higiyanu la-z'man ha-zeh.

Praised be Thou, O Lord our God, King of the Universe, Who hast Kept Us in Life and Sustained Us, and Enabled Us to Reach this Season.

While reclining to the left, drink the first cup of wine.

2. U-r'ḥatz — Wash the Hands

Since the HAMOTZI (the blessing for bread preceding the meal) does not follow at this point, the usual blessing for washing the hands is omitted. It was an ancient custom in the East, especially among Jews, to wash their hands before eating. A pitcher of water with basin and towels may be passed around to the guests or, to save time, several containers of water and basins may be set at convenient places on the table.

3. Karpas — Eat a Green Vegetable

The Haggadah preserves some of the customs extant when the Temple was still in existence in Jerusalem. All formal dinners began with an hors d'oeuvre. KARPAS is the hors d'oeuvre or appetizer of the Passover meal. It may consist of any green vegetable: parsley, lettuce, endive, cress, chervil, or scallion.

The green vegetable is a symbol of springtime and the miracle of nature's renewal. At this season when Mother Earth arrays herself in fresh verdure, the spirit of man rises, and he renews his faith in a world where freedom and justice will prevail.

The salt water into which the KARPAS is dipped to make it palatable, has been interpreted as salty tears, to remind us of the tears shed by the oppressed Israelites.

Before partaking of the KARPAS, recite the following blessing:

בָּרוּךְ אַתָּה, יְיָ אֱלֹהֵינוּ, מֶלֶךְ הָעוֹלָם, בּוֹרֵא פְּרִי הָאֲדָמָה.

Baruḥ atta Adonai elohenu meleḥ ha-olam, boray p'ri ha-adamah.

Praised Be Thou, O Lord our God, King of the Universe, Creator of the Fruit of the Earth.

4. Yaḥatz — BREAK THE MIDDLE OF THE THREE MATZOT

For the daily meal, there is one loaf of bread; but on the Sabbath there are two loaves as a reminder of the double portion of manna which fell on Friday for the Children of Israel as they traveled in the wilderness. (Ex. 16:22) In honor of Passover, a third matzah was added specifically for the Seder. The uppermost matzah is called KOHEN; the middle one, LEVI; and the third, YISRAEL. These represent the three classifications of Jews in ancient Judea.

When the Temple was in existence, special food, considered sacred, was eaten by the KOHANIM and the L'VI-YIM. But the Passover indicates that all Jews are united in a covenant of equality. To demonstrate this pattern of democracy, everyone at the Seder will tonight partake of all three matzot.

The middle matzah is broken into two pieces. The smaller half is replaced on the Seder plate to be used later for the HA-MOTZI. The larger half is wrapped in a napkin, as a symbol of the unleavened dough, to be eaten as the AFIKOMAN at the end of the meal. The Host, or Leader asks the children to close their eyes as he hides the AFIKOMAN. Anyone finding it may claim a reward because the meal cannot be ritually completed without the AFIKOMAN.

5. Maggid — TELL THE STORY OF THE EXODUS

Hospitality is a time-honored virtue among our people. The custom of inviting to the Seder all who are hungry, originated in Babylonia. Therefore the invitation is expressed not in Hebrew but in Aramaic, the language then current. Our Seder would not be true to tradition unless we offer hospitality to any stranger in our midst, or make it possible for the needy to observe their own Seder. Hence, the importance of the MAOT ḤITTIM Fund, which supplies Passover food to the poor in any local community and in other lands.

Mindful of the Jews' long years of persecution and wandering, let us bend every effort to help in the rebuilding of Zion so that our people shall nevermore be homeless nor oppressed, but have a homeland where they may live in dignity and freedom.

As we celebrate our Seder as free men in a free land, let us pray for the day when all men shall be free, free from poverty, free from fear, free from bigotry and free from the ravages of war.

Behold the MATZAH, bread of poverty, which our ancestors ate in the land of Egypt.

לַחְמָא עַנְיָא דִי אֲכָלוּ אַבְהָתָנָא בְּאַרְעָא דְמִצְרֶיִם.

Let all who are hungry come and eat; all who are needy, come and celebrate the Passover with us.

כָּל דִּכְפִין יֵיתֵי וְיֵיכָל, כָּל דִּצְרִיךְ יֵיתֵי וְיִפְסַח.

Now we are here; next year may we observe the Passover in the Land of Israel.

הָשַׁתָּא הָכָא, לְשָׁנָה הַבָּאָה בְּאַרְעָא דְיִשְׂרָאֵל.

Now many are still enslaved; next year may all men be free.

הָשַׁתָּא עַבְדֵי, לְשָׁנָה הַבָּאָה בְּנֵי חוֹרִין.

Ha lahma anya di ahalu avhatana b'ara d'mitzrayim. Kol dihfin yai-tai ve-yai-hul kol ditzrih yai-tai ve-yifsah. Ha-shata haha leshanah haba-a be-ara d'yisra-el. Ha-shata avdai leshanah haba-a b'nai horin.

7

The Haggadah, the dramatic portrayal of the exodus from Egyptian bondage, is for the entire family. Being child-centered, it encourages especially the children to ask questions concerning the ritual and meaning of the service. The Seder brings families together and strengthens the bonds of Jewish family solidarity.

After the door has been closed, the wine cup is filled the second time, and the youngest child, or a guest asks the Four Questions.

אַרְבַּע הַקֻּשִׁיוֹת

THE FOUR QUESTIONS

Why is this night different from all other nights?

נִשְׁתַּנָּה הַלַּיְלָה הַזֶּה מִכָּל הַלֵּילוֹת?

(1) On all other nights we may eat either leavened or unleavened bread, but on this night, only unleavened bread.

(1) שֶׁבְּכָל הַלֵּילוֹת אָנוּ אוֹכְלִין חָמֵץ וּמַצָּה, הַלַּיְלָה הַזֶּה כֻּלּוֹ מַצָּה.

(2) On all other nights we eat all kinds of herbs, but on this night we eat especially bitter herbs.

(2) שֶׁבְּכָל הַלֵּילוֹת אָנוּ אוֹכְלִין שְׁאָר יְרָקוֹת, הַלַּיְלָה הַזֶּה מָרוֹר.

(3) On all other nights, we need not even once dip our herbs in any condiment, but on this night we dip herbs twice: one herb in salt water, and the bitter herbs in ḤAROSET.

(3) שֶׁבְּכָל הַלֵּילוֹת אֵין אָנוּ מַטְבִּילִין אֲפִילוּ פַּעַם אֶחָת, הַלַּיְלָה הַזֶּה שְׁתֵּי פְעָמִים.

(4) On all other nights we eat either sitting or reclining, but on this night we recline.

(4) שֶׁבְּכָל הַלֵּילוֹת אָנוּ אוֹכְלִין בֵּין יוֹשְׁבִין וּבֵין מְסֻבִּין, הַלַּיְלָה הַזֶּה כֻּלָּנוּ מְסֻבִּין.

Before we read the Haggadah, which tells in detail the whole story, let me answer your questions one by one:

(1) We eat matzah because, when our ancestors were told by Pharaoh that they could leave Egypt, they had no time to bake bread with leaven, so they baked it without leaven.

(2) At the Seder, we eat bitter herbs to remind us of the bitterness our ancestors experienced when they were oppressed by the Egyptian taskmasters.

(3) At the Seder, we dip food twice: the parsley in salt water, as we have already explained, and the bitter herbs in ḤAROSET, as we shall later explain.

(4) As a sign of freedom, we lean to the left when we partake of wine and symbolic food. In antiquity, slaves ate hurriedly, standing or squatting on the ground, while royalty, nobility, and the wealthy in Egypt, Persia, Rome and other empires, dined on couches. To indicate that the ancient Israelites were now free, they too reclined while eating. Since it is impractical for each person to have a dining couch, the Leader is provided with pillows on which to lean, and the rest lean to the left when drinking the wine and eating the matzah.

Now let us return to the text of the Haggadah for the details as to why this night is different from all other nights. Whereas there are those who would like to conceal and forget their lowly origin, we Jews are constantly reminded of it. Not only at the Seder, but when we chant the Kiddush on Sabbaths and Festivals, when we read the Ten Commandments, and especially when we say our daily prayers, we recall that our ancestors were slaves in Egypt and were liberated by God. This constant reminder makes us cognizant that God works not only through nature but through history. It helps us to appreciate the importance of freedom and impresses upon us our responsibility to strive for the freedom of all men.

We were once the slaves of Pharaoh in Egypt, but the Lord our God brought us forth from there with a mighty hand and an outstretched arm. (Deut. 6:21; 26:8) Had not the Holy One, praised be He, brought our fathers out of Egypt, then we and our children and our children's children might still be enslaved to a Pharaoh in Egypt. Therefore, even if all of us were endowed with wisdom and understanding, and all of us thoroughly versed in the Torah, it would nevertheless be our duty to tell of the exodus from Egypt. And to dwell at length on the story of this liberation is indeed praiseworthy.

עֲבָדִים הָיִינוּ לְפַרְעֹה בְּמִצְרַיִם, וַיּוֹצִיאֵנוּ יְיָ אֱלֹהֵינוּ מִשָּׁם בְּיָד חֲזָקָה וּבִזְרוֹעַ נְטוּיָה. וְאִלּוּ לֹא הוֹצִיא הַקָּדוֹשׁ בָּרוּךְ הוּא אֶת אֲבוֹתֵינוּ מִמִּצְרַיִם, הֲרֵי אָנוּ וּבָנֵינוּ, וּבְנֵי בָנֵינוּ, מְשֻׁעְבָּדִים הָיִינוּ לְפַרְעֹה בְּמִצְרָיִם. וַאֲפִילוּ כֻּלָּנוּ חֲכָמִים, כֻּלָּנוּ נְבוֹנִים, כֻּלָּנוּ זְקֵנִים, כֻּלָּנוּ יוֹדְעִים אֶת הַתּוֹרָה, מִצְוָה עָלֵינוּ לְסַפֵּר בִּיצִיאַת מִצְרָיִם. וְכָל הַמַּרְבֶּה לְסַפֵּר בִּיצִיאַת מִצְרַיִם הֲרֵי זֶה מְשֻׁבָּח.

10

The following incident, of which the Haggadah is the only source, tells of a discussion by five Talmudic scholars, among whom Akiba was the most outstanding. Would that we had a transcript of that night-long conference and round-table talk!* B'nai B'rak, flourishing today near Tel Aviv, may be the very site of the ancient school of learning where the five Rabbis met.

We are told that Rabbi Eliezer, Rabbi Joshua, Rabbi Elazar, son of Azariah, Rabbi Akiba, and Rabbi Tarfon sat at the Seder table in B'nai B'rak and, the whole night through, discussed the liberation from Egypt until their disciples came in and said: "Rabbis! It is now time to recite the SHEMA of the morning prayers."

מַעֲשֶׂה בְּרַבִּי אֱלִיעֶזֶר וְרַבִּי יְהוֹשֻׁעַ, וְרַבִּי אֶלְעָזָר בֶּן עֲזַרְיָה וְרַבִּי עֲקִיבָא וְרַבִּי טַרְפוֹן, שֶׁהָיוּ מְסֻבִּין בִּבְנֵי בְרַק, וְהָיוּ מְסַפְּרִים בִּיצִיאַת מִצְרַיִם כָּל אוֹתוֹ הַלַּיְלָה, עַד שֶׁבָּאוּ תַלְמִידֵיהֶם וְאָמְרוּ לָהֶם: רַבּוֹתֵינוּ, הִגִּיעַ זְמַן קְרִיאַת שְׁמַע שֶׁל שַׁחֲרִית.

If great scholars could find the theme of freedom so fascinating that it kept them up all Seder night, we hope that our Seder will be made more meaningful by questions, comments and discussion on this theme.

That the Haggadah was an outgrowth of the discussion of the Sages is clearly indicated by the following passages:

Rabbi Elazar, son of Azariah, said, "I am nearly seventy years old, yet I never could understand why the exodus from Egypt should also be mentioned in the evening service, until Ben Zoma explained it by quoting the verse: 'That you may remember the day you went forth from Egypt all the days of your life. (Deut. 16:3) The days of your life would imply the daytime only. *All* the days of your life, includes the nights also.' " There is, however, another explanation given by the Sages: "The days of your life refers to this world. *All* the days of your life includes also the Messianic era."

אָמַר רַבִּי אֶלְעָזָר בֶּן עֲזַרְיָה: הֲרֵי אֲנִי כְּבֶן שִׁבְעִים שָׁנָה, וְלֹא זָכִיתִי שֶׁתֵּאָמֵר יְצִיאַת מִצְרַיִם בַּלֵּילוֹת, עַד שֶׁדְּרָשָׁהּ בֶּן זוֹמָא, שֶׁנֶּאֱמַר: לְמַעַן תִּזְכֹּר אֶת יוֹם צֵאתְךָ מֵאֶרֶץ מִצְרַיִם כֹּל יְמֵי חַיֶּיךָ. יְמֵי חַיֶּיךָ הַיָּמִים; כֹּל יְמֵי חַיֶּיךָ הַלֵּילוֹת. וַחֲכָמִים אוֹמְרִים: יְמֵי חַיֶּיךָ הָעוֹלָם הַזֶּה; כֹּל יְמֵי חַיֶּיךָ לְהָבִיא לִימוֹת הַמָּשִׁיחַ.

---

* It has been suggested by the author of a fascinating book on the life of Akiba, that these scholars were planning a revolt against the Romans who had proscribed, under penalty of death, the study of the Torah.

Praised be God; praised be He; praised be He who gave the Torah to His people Israel; praised be He.

בָּרוּךְ הַמָּקוֹם, בָּרוּךְ הוּא. בָּרוּךְ שֶׁנָּתַן תּוֹרָה לְעַמּוֹ יִשְׂרָאֵל, בָּרוּךְ הוּא.

Four times the Torah declares that a father should tell his son the story of Passover (Ex. 12:26; 13:8; 13:14; and Deut. 6:20). Thus the Sages infer that there are four types of children:

(1) The ḤAKHAM, variously translated as wise, clever, intelligent or mature;

(2) the RASHA, not wicked in the sense of an evildoer, but rebellious, scornful, stubborn and contemptuous, who does not inquire, and is irreverent and defiant;

(3) the TAM, the dull, simple, immature child;

(4) the SHE-ENO YO-DE-A LISH-OL, the child not yet capable of inquiring.

THE FOUR SONS

The Torah speaks of four types of children: one who is wise, one who is rebellious, one who is simple, and one who does not know how to ask.

כְּנֶגֶד אַרְבָּעָה בָנִים דִּבְּרָה תוֹרָה: אֶחָד חָכָם, וְאֶחָד רָשָׁע, וְאֶחָד תָּם, וְאֶחָד שֶׁאֵינוֹ יוֹדֵעַ לִשְׁאוֹל.

THE WISE SON asks, "What is the meaning of the laws, regulations and ordinances which the Lord our God has commanded you?" (Deut. 6:20) To him you shall explain all the laws of Passover even to the last detail, that nothing may be eaten and no entertainment or revelry is to take place after the AFIKOMAN.

חָכָם מַה הוּא אוֹמֵר: מָה הָעֵדֹת וְהַחֻקִּים וְהַמִּשְׁפָּטִים אֲשֶׁר צִוָּה יְיָ אֱלֹהֵינוּ אֶתְכֶם: וְאַף אַתָּה אֱמָר לוֹ כְּהִלְכוֹת הַפֶּסַח, אֵין מַפְטִירִין אַחַר הַפֶּסַח אֲפִיקוֹמָן.

12

THE REBELLIOUS SON asks: "What does this service mean to you?" (Ex. 12:26) By using the expression "to you," it is evident that this service has no significance for *him*. He has thus excluded himself from his people and denied God; therefore, give him a caustic answer and say: "It is because of what the Lord did for *me* when I came out of Egypt." (Ex. 13:8) "For me," not for *him*, for had he been there in Egypt, he would not have deserved to be liberated.

רָשָׁע מַה הוּא אוֹמֵר: מָה הָעֲבֹדָה הַזֹּאת לָכֶם? לָכֶם וְלֹא לוֹ. וּלְפִי שֶׁהוֹצִיא אֶת עַצְמוֹ מִן הַכְּלָל כָּפַר בָּעִקָּר. וְאַף אַתָּה הַקְהֵה אֶת שִׁנָּיו, וֶאֱמָר לוֹ: בַּעֲבוּר זֶה עָשָׂה יְיָ לִי בְּצֵאתִי מִמִּצְרָיִם. לִי וְלֹא לוֹ, אִלּוּ הָיָה שָׁם לֹא הָיָה נִגְאָל.

The SIMPLE SON asks: "What does this mean?" Tell him, "With a mighty hand, the Lord brought us out of Egypt, out of the house of bondage." (Ex. 13:14)

תָּם מַה הוּא אוֹמֵר: מַה זֹּאת? וְאָמַרְתָּ אֵלָיו: בְּחֹזֶק יָד הוֹצִיאָנוּ יְיָ מִמִּצְרַיִם, מִבֵּית עֲבָדִים.

13

AS FOR THE ONE WHO DOES NOT KNOW HOW TO ASK, begin by explaining, as we are told: "You shall tell your son on that day,* 'I do this because of what the Lord did for me when I came out of Egypt.'" (Ex. 13:8)

One might think that the Haggadah should be recited beginning with the first day of the month of Nisan. But the Bible says: "You shall tell your son *on that day*," (the fifteenth day of Nisan, the first day of Passover). One might infer *on that day* means in the daytime. But the verse continues: "I do this because of what the Lord did for me when I came out of Egypt," namely in the evening, when the matzah and bitter herbs are actually placed before you.

וְשֶׁאֵינוֹ יוֹדֵעַ לִשְׁאוֹל – אַתְּ פְּתַח לוֹ, שֶׁנֶּאֱמַר: וְהִגַּדְתָּ לְבִנְךָ בַּיּוֹם הַהוּא לֵאמֹר: בַּעֲבוּר זֶה עָשָׂה יְיָ לִי בְּצֵאתִי מִמִּצְרָיִם.

יָכֹל מֵרֹאשׁ חֹדֶשׁ, תַּלְמוּד לוֹמַר: בַּיּוֹם הַהוּא. אִי בַּיּוֹם הַהוּא, יָכֹל מִבְּעוֹד יוֹם, תַּלְמוּד לוֹמַר: בַּעֲבוּר זֶה. בַּעֲבוּר זֶה לֹא אָמַרְתִּי אֶלָּא בְּשָׁעָה שֶׁיֵּשׁ מַצָּה וּמָרוֹר מֻנָּחִים לְפָנֶיךָ.

In accordance with the requirement that the reply to the Four Questions should begin with "the humiliation of a people and end with its glory," Samuel, head of the Nehardea Academy, preferred the opening passage to be, "We were once slaves of Pharaoh in Egypt," whereas Rav, head of the Sura Academy, advocated the passage, "Our forefathers were idol worshipers." (Pesaḥim 116a) Both of these passages have been included, and are interpreted to refer to two kinds of slavery from which the Israelites were emancipated: the first, that of physical bondage; the second, that of spiritual bondage. It is not enough to be free in body; one must be

---

* Because the pronoun "You" in the verse, "You shall tell your son" is *aht*, feminine, it has been interpreted that it is the mother who shall impart the first instruction to the child.

free also in mind. Jews have frequently been threatened with both kinds of slavery — the slavery imposed from without, which sought to destroy the Jews physically, and the self-imposed slavery which destroyed spiritually those Jews who turned from God and repudiated the religion and traditions of their fathers.

In the beginning (before the days of Abraham), our forefathers were idol worshipers. God, however, called us to His service. For so we read in the Torah: "And Joshua said unto all the people, 'Thus said the Lord, God of Israel: In the days of old, your fathers, even Teraḥ, the father of Abraham and Naḥor, lived beyond the River Euphrates, and they worshiped idols. But I took your father, Abraham, from beyond the River Euphrates and I led him through the entire land of Canaan. I multiplied his offspring and gave him Isaac. To Isaac I gave Jacob and Esau. To Esau I gave Mount Seir as an inheritance; but Jacob and his sons went down into Egypt.' " (Josh. 24:2–4)

Praised be God who keeps His promise to Israel; praised be He! For the Holy One, praised be He, determined the end of our bondage in order to fulfill His word, pledged in a solemn covenant to our father Abraham: "And God said to Abram, 'Know this for certain: your descendants shall be strangers in a land not their own, where they shall be enslaved and oppressed for four hundred years. But I will also bring judgment on the nation that held them in slavery; and in the end they shall go free with great substance.' " (Gen. 15:13, 14)

תְּחִלָּה עוֹבְדֵי עֲבוֹדָה זָרָה הָיוּ אֲבוֹתֵינוּ, וְעַכְשָׁו קֵרְבָנוּ הַמָּקוֹם לַעֲבוֹדָתוֹ, שֶׁנֶּאֱמַר: וַיֹּאמֶר יְהוֹשֻׁעַ אֶל כָּל הָעָם, כֹּה אָמַר יְיָ אֱלֹהֵי יִשְׂרָאֵל, בְּעֵבֶר הַנָּהָר יָשְׁבוּ אֲבוֹתֵיכֶם מֵעוֹלָם, תֶּרַח אֲבִי אַבְרָהָם וַאֲבִי נָחוֹר; וַיַּעַבְדוּ אֱלֹהִים אֲחֵרִים. וָאֶקַּח אֶת אֲבִיכֶם אֶת אַבְרָהָם מֵעֵבֶר הַנָּהָר, וָאוֹלֵךְ אוֹתוֹ בְּכָל אֶרֶץ כְּנָעַן; וָאַרְבֶּה אֶת זַרְעוֹ, וָאֶתֵּן לוֹ אֶת יִצְחָק. וָאֶתֵּן לְיִצְחָק אֶת יַעֲקֹב וְאֶת עֵשָׂו; וָאֶתֵּן לְעֵשָׂו אֶת הַר שֵׂעִיר לָרֶשֶׁת אוֹתוֹ, וְיַעֲקֹב וּבָנָיו יָרְדוּ מִצְרָיִם.

בָּרוּךְ שׁוֹמֵר הַבְטָחָתוֹ לְיִשְׂרָאֵל, בָּרוּךְ הוּא. שֶׁהַקָּדוֹשׁ בָּרוּךְ הוּא חִשַּׁב אֶת הַקֵּץ לַעֲשׂוֹת כְּמוֹ שֶׁאָמַר לְאַבְרָהָם אָבִינוּ בִּבְרִית בֵּין הַבְּתָרִים, שֶׁנֶּאֱמַר: וַיֹּאמֶר לְאַבְרָם, יָדֹעַ תֵּדַע כִּי גֵר יִהְיֶה זַרְעֲךָ בְּאֶרֶץ לֹא לָהֶם, וַעֲבָדוּם וְעִנּוּ אֹתָם, אַרְבַּע מֵאוֹת שָׁנָה. וְגַם אֶת הַגּוֹי אֲשֶׁר יַעֲבֹדוּ דָּן אָנֹכִי; וְאַחֲרֵי כֵן יֵצְאוּ בִּרְכֻשׁ גָּדוֹל.

15

Our Sages found meaning in every word and letter of the ancient text. For example, in the following prayer, they thus interpreted the first word, v'HI: the VAV has the numerical value of six, and signifies the six divisions of the Mishnah; the HEH, the Five Books of Moses; the YOD, the Ten Commandments; and the ALEF, the one God.

Raise the cup of wine and cover the matzot.

God's unfailing help has sustained our fathers and us. For not only one enemy has risen up to destroy us, but in every generation do men rise up against us seeking to destroy us; but the Holy One, praised be He, delivers us from their hands.

הִיא שֶׁעָמְדָה לַאֲבוֹתֵינוּ וְלָנוּ. שֶׁלֹּא אֶחָד בִּלְבָד, עָמַד עָלֵינוּ לְכַלּוֹתֵינוּ, אֶלָּא שֶׁבְּכָל דּוֹר וָדוֹר עוֹמְדִים עָלֵינוּ לְכַלּוֹתֵנוּ, וְהַקָּדוֹשׁ בָּרוּךְ הוּא מַצִּילֵנוּ מִיָּדָם.

The cup of wine is set down on the table and the matzot are uncovered.

We must be on guard against two kinds of enemies who would deprive us of our freedom: (1) the enemy without, easily recognized by his malicious words and evil deeds; and (2) the enemy within, posing as a friend and betraying us. Pharaoh was the enemy without and Laban, referred to in the passage which follows, symbolized the treacherous, false friend. By transposing the letters of the word אֲרַמִּי ARAMI (Aramean) it becomes רַמַּאי RAMAI, which means deceitful. In Jewish legend, Laban the Aramean (Syrian), not only attempted to annihilate Jacob and his descendants, but also incited others to destroy Israel.

It seems strange that Laban should be regarded as a greater menace to Israel than Pharaoh. A modern scholar maintains that this interpretation was given in the third century B. C. E., when Syria (Aram), typified by Laban, and Egypt, typified by Pharaoh, were rivals for the control of Palestine, then ruled by the Egyptian Ptolemies. Since the Haggadah is not favorable to Egypt, this Midrash was introduced as a gesture of good will towards the Egyptians, with whom the Jews of Palestine desired to live on friendly terms.

Let us analyze, for instance, what Laban, the Aramean (Syrian), intended to do to Jacob, our father. Whereas Pharaoh issued a decree against new-born males only, Laban sought to annihilate Jacob and his entire family, for the Biblical verse may be read: "The Aramean wanted to destroy my father."

צֵא וּלְמַד, מַה בִּקֵּשׁ לָבָן הָאֲרַמִּי לַעֲשׂוֹת לְיַעֲקֹב אָבִינוּ. שֶׁפַּרְעֹה לֹא גָזַר אֶלָּא עַל הַזְּכָרִים, וְלָבָן בִּקֵּשׁ לַעֲקֹר אֶת הַכֹּל, שֶׁנֶּאֱמַר: אֲרַמִּי אֹבֵד אָבִי.

What follows is the Midrashic interpretation in rabbinic style of four Biblical verses (Deut. 26:5–8) referring to the history of Israel and Egypt. These verses form part of a ritual annually recited by our ancestors when, at Shavuot, they brought their first fruits to the Temple at Jerusalem. Each word or phrase is critically analyzed and elaborated, and the Haggadah is the only source of this ancient exposition.

(1) "The Aramean wanted to destroy my father, but my father went down to Egypt and he sojourned there; (his household was) few in number, and there he became a nation, great, mighty and populous." (Deut. 26:5)

(1) אֲרַמִּי אֹבֵד אָבִי, וַיֵּרֶד מִצְרַיְמָה, וַיָּגָר שָׁם בִּמְתֵי מְעָט; וַיְהִי שָׁם לְגוֹי גָּדוֹל, עָצוּם וָרָב.

"He went down to Egypt": compelled to do so by divine command.

וַיֵּרֶד מִצְרַיְמָה: אָנוּס עַל פִּי הַדִּבּוּר.

"And sojourned there": from which we learn that Jacob did not intend to settle in Egypt, but only to dwell there temporarily, for the verse reads, "And the sons of Jacob said to Pharaoh, 'We have come to the land to dwell here temporarily, as there is no pasture for your servants' flocks, for the famine is severe in Canaan. Let then your servants dwell in the land of Goshen.'" (Gen. 47:4)

וַיָּגָר שָׁם: מְלַמֵּד שֶׁלֹּא יָרַד יַעֲקֹב אָבִינוּ לְהִשְׁתַּקֵּעַ בְּמִצְרַיִם אֶלָּא לָגוּר שָׁם, שֶׁנֶּאֱמַר, וַיֹּאמְרוּ אֶל פַּרְעֹה, לָגוּר בָּאָרֶץ בָּאנוּ, כִּי אֵין מִרְעֶה לַצֹּאן אֲשֶׁר לַעֲבָדֶיךָ, כִּי כָבֵד הָרָעָב בְּאֶרֶץ כְּנָעַן; וְעַתָּה יֵשְׁבוּ נָא עֲבָדֶיךָ בְּאֶרֶץ גֹּשֶׁן.

"Few in number": (as Moses said to the Children of Israel), "With only seventy souls your fathers went down to Egypt; and now the Lord your God has made you as numerous as the stars of the heaven." (Deut. 10:22)

בִּמְתֵי מְעָט: כְּמוֹ שֶׁנֶּאֱמַר, בְּשִׁבְעִים נֶפֶשׁ יָרְדוּ אֲבֹתֶיךָ מִצְרָיְמָה; וְעַתָּה שָׂמְךָ יְיָ אֱלֹהֶיךָ כְּכוֹכְבֵי הַשָּׁמַיִם לָרֹב.

"And there he became a nation": indicating that even then the Israelites were identified as a distinct people.

וַיְהִי שָׁם לְגוֹי: מְלַמֵּד שֶׁהָיוּ יִשְׂרָאֵל מְצֻיָּנִים שָׁם.

"Great and mighty": as we read, "And the Children of Israel were fruitful, and increased abundantly, and multiplied, and became great and mighty; and the land was filled with them." (Ex. 1:7)

גָּדוֹל, עָצוּם: כְּמוֹ שֶׁנֶּאֱמַר, וּבְנֵי יִשְׂרָאֵל פָּרוּ וַיִּשְׁרְצוּ, וַיִּרְבּוּ וַיַּעַצְמוּ בִּמְאֹד מְאֹד; וַתִּמָּלֵא הָאָרֶץ אֹתָם.

"And populous": as it is written in the Book of Ezekiel (16:7), "I have caused you to multiply as the buds of the field; you did multiply and grow in stature and beauty; your breasts were fashioned and your hair grew long; yet you were naked and bare."

(Though the Israelites had developed physically in Egypt, they were still spiritually immature because they had not yet received the Torah.)

וָרָב: כְּמוֹ שֶׁנֶּאֱמַר, רְבָבָה כְּצֶמַח הַשָּׂדֶה נְתַתִּיךְ; וַתִּרְבִּי וַתִּגְדְּלִי, וַתָּבֹאִי בַּעֲדִי עֲדָיִים; שָׁדַיִם נָכֹנוּ, וּשְׂעָרֵךְ צִמֵּחַ, וְאַתְּ עֵרֹם וְעֶרְיָה.

17

(2) "And the Egyptians treated us harshly and oppressed us, and imposed hard labor upon us." (Deut. 26:6)

"And the Egyptians treated us harshly": for as Pharaoh said, "Come let us outwit them lest they multiply and, in the event that we have war, they will join our enemies and fight against us, and escape from our land." (Ex. 1:10)

"And oppressed us": for the Bible tells us, "So the Egyptians appointed taskmasters over them to oppress them with heavy burdens; and the Israelites built for Pharaoh the treasure cities of Pithom and Raamses." (Ex. 1:11)

"And they imposed hard labor upon us": as it is written, "The Egyptians imposed hard labor upon the Children of Israel." (Ex. 1:13)

(3) "And we cried unto the Lord, the God of our fathers, and the Lord heard our cry, and saw our affliction, our travail and our oppression." (Deut. 26:7)

"And we cried unto the Lord, the God of our fathers": as the Bible tells us, "When many years had passed and the king of Egypt died, the Children of Israel moaned because of their bondage, and they cried; and from the midst of their slavery their cry came up to God." (Ex. 2:23)

"And the Lord heard our cry": as the verse relates, "God heard their groaning and God remembered His covenant with Abraham, with Isaac, and with Jacob." (Ex. 2:24)

"And He saw our affliction": this phrase refers to the enforced separation of husbands and wives. This is the interpretation of the verse, "And God saw the Children of Israel, and God knew their plight." (Ex. 2:25)

(2) וַיָּרֵעוּ אֹתָנוּ הַמִּצְרִים וַיְעַנּוּנוּ,
וַיִּתְּנוּ עָלֵינוּ עֲבֹדָה קָשָׁה.

וַיָּרֵעוּ אֹתָנוּ הַמִּצְרִים: כְּמוֹ שֶׁנֶּאֱמַר,
הָבָה נִתְחַכְּמָה לוֹ, פֶּן יִרְבֶּה, וְהָיָה כִּי
תִקְרֶאנָה מִלְחָמָה, וְנוֹסַף גַּם הוּא עַל שֹׂנְאֵינוּ
וְנִלְחַם בָּנוּ וְעָלָה מִן הָאָרֶץ.

וַיְעַנּוּנוּ: כְּמוֹ שֶׁנֶּאֱמַר, וַיָּשִׂימוּ עָלָיו שָׂרֵי
מִסִּים, לְמַעַן עַנֹּתוֹ בְּסִבְלֹתָם. וַיִּבֶן עָרֵי
מִסְכְּנוֹת לְפַרְעֹה, אֶת פִּתֹם וְאֶת רַעַמְסֵס.

וַיִּתְּנוּ עָלֵינוּ עֲבֹדָה קָשָׁה: כְּמוֹ שֶׁנֶּאֱמַר,
וַיַּעֲבִדוּ מִצְרַיִם אֶת בְּנֵי יִשְׂרָאֵל בְּפָרֶךְ.

(3) וַנִּצְעַק אֶל יְיָ אֱלֹהֵי אֲבֹתֵינוּ;
וַיִּשְׁמַע יְיָ אֶת קֹלֵנוּ, וַיַּרְא אֶת עָנְיֵנוּ,
וְאֶת עֲמָלֵנוּ וְאֶת לַחֲצֵנוּ.

וַנִּצְעַק אֶל יְיָ אֱלֹהֵי אֲבוֹתֵינוּ: כְּמוֹ
שֶׁנֶּאֱמַר, וַיְהִי בַיָּמִים הָרַבִּים הָהֵם, וַיָּמָת
מֶלֶךְ מִצְרַיִם, וַיֵּאָנְחוּ בְנֵי יִשְׂרָאֵל מִן הָעֲבֹדָה
וַיִּזְעָקוּ; וַתַּעַל שַׁוְעָתָם אֶל הָאֱלֹהִים מִן
הָעֲבֹדָה.

וַיִּשְׁמַע יְיָ אֶת קֹלֵנוּ: כְּמוֹ שֶׁנֶּאֱמַר, וַיִּשְׁמַע
אֱלֹהִים אֶת נַאֲקָתָם, וַיִּזְכֹּר אֱלֹהִים אֶת
בְּרִיתוֹ אֶת אַבְרָהָם, אֶת יִצְחָק וְאֶת יַעֲקֹב.

וַיַּרְא אֶת עָנְיֵנוּ: זוֹ פְּרִישׁוּת דֶּרֶךְ אֶרֶץ,
כְּמוֹ שֶׁנֶּאֱמַר, וַיַּרְא אֱלֹהִים אֶת בְּנֵי יִשְׂרָאֵל,
וַיֵּדַע אֱלֹהִים.

18

"And our travail": this recalls the drowning of the children, as it is written, "Every son that is born you shall cast into the Nile, but every daughter you may allow to live." (Ex. 1:22)

וְאֶת עֲמָלֵנוּ: אֵלּוּ הַבָּנִים, כְּמוֹ שֶׁנֶּאֱמַר, כָּל הַבֵּן הַיִּלּוֹד הַיְאֹרָה תַּשְׁלִיכֻהוּ, וְכָל הַבַּת תְּחַיּוּן.

"And our oppression": this refers to their persecution, of which the Bible says, "I have also seen the oppression wherewith the Egyptians oppressed them." (Ex. 3:9)

וְאֶת לַחֲצֵנוּ: זֶה הַדְּחַק, כְּמוֹ שֶׁנֶּאֱמַר, וְגַם רָאִיתִי אֶת הַלַּחַץ אֲשֶׁר מִצְרַיִם לֹחֲצִים אֹתָם.

(4) "And the Lord brought us out of Egypt with a mighty hand, with outstretched arm, in the midst of great awe, signs, and wonders." (Deut. 26:8)

(4) וַיּוֹצִאֵנוּ יְיָ מִמִּצְרַיִם, בְּיָד חֲזָקָה וּבִזְרֹעַ נְטוּיָה, וּבְמֹרָא גָּדֹל, וּבְאֹתוֹת וּבְמֹפְתִים.

"And the Lord brought us out of Egypt": not by any intermediary angel, seraph, or messenger, but by God Himself, in His glory, the Holy One, praised be He. For the Bible records, "I will pass through the land of Egypt on that night and I will smite all the first-born in the land of Egypt, both man and beast, and I will execute judgments against all the gods of Egypt. I am the Lord." (Ex. 12:12)

וַיּוֹצִאֵנוּ יְיָ מִמִּצְרַיִם: לֹא עַל יְדֵי מַלְאָךְ, וְלֹא עַל יְדֵי שָׂרָף, וְלֹא עַל יְדֵי שָׁלִיחַ, אֶלָּא הַקָּדוֹשׁ בָּרוּךְ הוּא בִּכְבוֹדוֹ וּבְעַצְמוֹ, שֶׁנֶּאֱמַר, וְעָבַרְתִּי בְאֶרֶץ מִצְרַיִם בַּלַּיְלָה הַזֶּה, וְהִכֵּיתִי כָל בְּכוֹר בְּאֶרֶץ מִצְרַיִם, מֵאָדָם וְעַד בְּהֵמָה; וּבְכָל אֱלֹהֵי מִצְרַיִם אֶעֱשֶׂה שְׁפָטִים, אֲנִי יְיָ.

"I will pass through the land of Egypt on that night": I, and not an angel; "I will smite all the first-born in the land of Egypt": I, and not a seraph. "And against all the gods of Egypt I will execute judgments": I, and not a messenger. "I am the Lord": I am He, there is no other.

וְעָבַרְתִּי בְאֶרֶץ מִצְרַיִם בַּלַּיְלָה הַזֶּה: אֲנִי וְלֹא מַלְאָךְ; וְהִכֵּיתִי כָל בְּכוֹר בְּאֶרֶץ מִצְרַיִם: אֲנִי וְלֹא שָׂרָף. וּבְכָל אֱלֹהֵי מִצְרַיִם אֶעֱשֶׂה שְׁפָטִים: אֲנִי וְלֹא הַשָּׁלִיחַ. אֲנִי יְיָ: אֲנִי הוּא וְלֹא אַחֵר.

"With a mighty hand": this refers to the cattle plague (even as Pharaoh was warned), "Behold the hand of the Lord will smite with a deadly pestilence your cattle in the field, your horses, donkeys, camels, herds and flocks." (Ex. 9:3)

בְּיָד חֲזָקָה: זוֹ הַדֶּבֶר, כְּמוֹ שֶׁנֶּאֱמַר, הִנֵּה יַד יְיָ הוֹיָה בְּמִקְנְךָ אֲשֶׁר בַּשָּׂדֶה, בַּסּוּסִים, בַּחֲמֹרִים, בַּגְּמַלִּים, בַּבָּקָר וּבַצֹּאן, דֶּבֶר כָּבֵד מְאֹד.

"And with outstretched arm": this suggests the sword of destruction as we read, "And the drawn sword in his hand, outstretched over Jerusalem." (1 Chron. 21:16)

וּבִזְרֹעַ נְטוּיָה: זוֹ הַחֶרֶב, כְּמוֹ שֶׁנֶּאֱמַר, וְחַרְבּוֹ שְׁלוּפָה בְּיָדוֹ, נְטוּיָה עַל יְרוּשָׁלָיִם.

19

"In the midst of great awe": this refers to the revelation of the Divine Presence. We understand this from the verse, "Has God ever sought to go and take for Himself a nation out of the midst of another nation, by trials, signs, wonders, war, by a mighty hand, outstretched arm, and by great awe, just as the Lord your God did for you, before your very eyes, in Egypt?" (Deut. 4:34)

"Signs": this alludes to the rod of Moses, as we are told, "Take this rod in your hand, and with it perform signs.' (Ex. 4:17)

"Wonders": this refers to the miracle where the water of Egypt turned into blood as we see from the verse, "I will show wonders in the heavens and on the earth:

וּבְמֹרָא גָדֹל: זוֹ גִלּוּי שְׁכִינָה, כְּמוֹ שֶׁנֶּאֱמַר, אוֹ הֲנִסָּה אֱלֹהִים, לָבוֹא לָקַחַת לוֹ גוֹי מִקֶּרֶב גּוֹי, בְּמַסֹּת, בְּאֹתֹת וּבְמוֹפְתִים וּבְמִלְחָמָה, וּבְיָד חֲזָקָה וּבִזְרוֹעַ נְטוּיָה, וּבְמוֹרָאִים גְּדֹלִים, כְּכֹל אֲשֶׁר עָשָׂה לָכֶם יְיָ אֱלֹהֵיכֶם, בְּמִצְרַיִם לְעֵינֶיךָ?

וּבְאֹתוֹת: זֶה הַמַּטֶּה, כְּמוֹ שֶׁנֶּאֱמַר, וְאֶת הַמַּטֶּה הַזֶּה תִּקַּח בְּיָדֶךָ, אֲשֶׁר תַּעֲשֶׂה בּוֹ אֶת הָאֹתֹת.

וּבְמֹפְתִים: זֶה הַדָּם, כְּמוֹ שֶׁנֶּאֱמַר, וְנָתַתִּי מוֹפְתִים בַּשָּׁמַיִם וּבָאָרֶץ:

With a small spoon, spill from your cup some wine for each of the three miracles.

Blood, fire, and pillars of smoke."
(Joel 3:3)

Another interpretation (of Deut. 26:8) is: *strong hand*, indicates two plagues; *out-stretched arm*, two plagues; *great awe*, two plagues; *signs* (since it is in the plural), two plagues; and *wonders* (in the plural), two plagues; thus making the ten plagues.

דָּם, וָאֵשׁ, וְתִמְרוֹת עָשָׁן.

דָּבָר אַחֵר: בְּיָד חֲזָקָה שְׁתַּיִם; וּבִזְרוֹעַ נְטוּיָה שְׁתַּיִם; וּבְמֹרָא גָדֹל שְׁתַּיִם; וּבְאֹתוֹת שְׁתַּיִם; וּבְמֹפְתִים שְׁתַּיִם.

LESS THAN FULL JOY

As we read in the Haggadah about plague after plague, with a small spoon we spill some wine into our plate. The Psalmist tells us: "Wine makes glad the heart of man." But how can we fully rejoice as we celebrate Israel's freedom when we know that our redemption involved the suffering of the Egyptians. We cannot be joyous when any human being, even an enemy, is afflicted. Hence, our second cup of joy cannot be full; the symbol of gladness is diminished by the wine we spill to express sorrow for the Egyptians. It may be for the same reason that the command "You shall rejoice" which occurs three times in reference to the Feast of Tabernacles (Lev. 23:40; Deut. 16:14, 15) is omitted in connection with Passover.

The Midrash relates that when the Egyptians were drowning in the Red Sea and the angels wanted to sing Halleluyah, God rebuked them: "How can you sing Halleluyah when My children are drowning?" (Megillah 10b) That is why only half Hallel (Songs of Praise), and not the full Hallel, is recited during the last six days of Passover. This is one of the numerous interpretations which refutes the libel that Jews are vindictive and do not know the meaning of love. In our Scriptures are contained many dictums expressing the Jewish emphasis on love. In the Five Books of Moses we are told: "Love thy neighbor as thyself." (Lev. 19:18) The Book of Proverbs cautions us: "Rejoice not when your enemy falls." (24:17)

In God's eyes all people are His children, and all nations His creation. "Have we not all one Father? Has not one God created us all?" (Mal. 2:10) "Are you not like the children of the Ethiopians unto Me, O Children of Israel?" says the Lord. (Amos 9:7)

With a small spoon, spill into your plate some of the wine as each plague is mentioned.

These were the ten plagues which the Holy One, praised be He, brought upon the Egyptians in Egypt:

אֵלּוּ עֶשֶׂר מַכּוֹת שֶׁהֵבִיא הַקָּדוֹשׁ בָּרוּךְ הוּא עַל הַמִּצְרִים בְּמִצְרַיִם, וְאֵלּוּ הֵן:

דָּם, צְפַרְדֵּעַ, כִּנִּים, עָרוֹב, דֶּבֶר, שְׁחִין, בָּרָד, אַרְבֶּה, חֹשֶׁךְ, מַכַּת בְּכֹרוֹת.

Dam, Tz'fardea, Kinnim, Arov, Dever,
Sh'ḥin, Barad, Arbeh, Ḥoshekh, Makat b'khorot.

(1) Blood, (2) Frogs, (3) Vermin, (4) Wild Beasts, (5) Cattle Disease, (6) Boils, (7) Hail, (8) Locusts, (9) Darkness, (10) Smiting of the First-Born.

To facilitate remembering the order of the ten plagues as they occurred, and to avoid mentioning them by name, Rabbi Judah put together the first Hebrew letter of each plague and formed three words.

As each of the three words is mentioned, spill some wine from your cup.

Rabbi Judah used to refer to these plagues as follows:

רַבִּי יְהוּדָה הָיָה נוֹתֵן בָּהֶם סִמָּנִים:

D'TZaKH, ADaSH, B'AHaB.

דְּצַ"ךְ, עֲדַ"שׁ, בְּאַחַ"ב.

21

In the spirit of the Haggadah that one should dwell at length on the story of the Exodus, scholars vie with one another in magnifying the number of miracles that occurred. In the following passages, the Sages interpreted verses to indicate that there were as many as two hundred and fifty plagues, thus magnifying the abundant mercy and protection of God in sparing the Israelites.

Rabbi Jose, the Galilean, asked how can one deduce that if the Egyptians were smitten with ten plagues in Egypt, they were smitten with fifty plagues at the Red Sea? Referring to the plagues in Egypt, the Bible says: "And the magicians said to Pharaoh, 'This is the *finger* of God.'" (Ex. 8:15) At the Red Sea, however, the Bible says: "And Israel saw the great *hand* which the Lord laid upon the Egyptians, and the people stood in awe of the Lord, and they believed in the Lord, and in His servant Moses." (Ex. 14:31) If, in Egypt, one finger of God caused ten plagues, then we may assume that at the Red Sea the whole hand of God brought fifty plagues.

רַבִּי יוֹסֵי הַגְּלִילִי אוֹמֵר: מִנַּיִן אַתָּה אוֹמֵר שֶׁלָּקוּ הַמִּצְרִים בְּמִצְרַיִם עֶשֶׂר מַכּוֹת, וְעַל הַיָּם לָקוּ חֲמִשִּׁים מַכּוֹת? בְּמִצְרַיִם מַה הוּא אוֹמֵר? וַיֹּאמְרוּ הַחַרְטֻמִּים אֶל פַּרְעֹה, אֶצְבַּע אֱלֹהִים הִיא. וְעַל הַיָּם מַה הוּא אוֹמֵר? וַיַּרְא יִשְׂרָאֵל אֶת הַיָּד הַגְּדוֹלָה אֲשֶׁר עָשָׂה יְיָ בְּמִצְרַיִם, וַיִּירְאוּ הָעָם אֶת יְיָ; וַיַּאֲמִינוּ בַּיְיָ וּבְמֹשֶׁה עַבְדּוֹ. כַּמָּה לָקוּ בָּאֶצְבַּע? עֶשֶׂר מַכּוֹת. אֱמוֹר מֵעַתָּה: בְּמִצְרַיִם לָקוּ עֶשֶׂר מַכּוֹת, וְעַל הַיָּם לָקוּ חֲמִשִּׁים מַכּוֹת.

Rabbi Eliezer asked how can you show that every plague which God visited upon the Egyptians was fourfold? We read in Psalms: "He sent against the Egyptians His burning anger: wrath, indignation, trouble, and messengers of evil." (78:49) "Wrath" indicates one; "indignation," two; "trouble," three; "messengers of evil," four. Therefore, if each plague is fourfold, in Egypt they were smitten with forty plagues, and at the Red Sea with two hundred.

רַבִּי אֱלִיעֶזֶר אוֹמֵר: מִנַּיִן שֶׁכָּל מַכָּה וּמַכָּה, שֶׁהֵבִיא הַקָּדוֹשׁ בָּרוּךְ הוּא עַל הַמִּצְרִים בְּמִצְרַיִם, הָיְתָה שֶׁל אַרְבַּע מַכּוֹת? שֶׁנֶּאֱמַר: יְשַׁלַּח בָּם חֲרוֹן אַפּוֹ, עֶבְרָה, וָזַעַם, וְצָרָה, מִשְׁלַחַת מַלְאֲכֵי רָעִים. עֶבְרָה אַחַת, וָזַעַם שְׁתַּיִם, וְצָרָה שָׁלֹשׁ, מִשְׁלַחַת מַלְאֲכֵי רָעִים אַרְבַּע. אֱמוֹר מֵעַתָּה: בְּמִצְרַיִם לָקוּ אַרְבָּעִים מַכּוֹת, וְעַל הַיָּם לָקוּ מָאתַיִם מַכּוֹת.

Rabbi Akiba went further, and asked how can one infer that every plague which God inflicted upon the Egyptians in Egypt was really fivefold? The same verse in Psalms may be interpreted as follows: "His burning anger" indicates one; "wrath," two; "indignation," three; "trouble," four; and "messengers of evil," five. Thus, if the Egyptians were stricken by the finger of God with fifty plagues, it follows that at the Red Sea they were stricken by the whole hand of God with two hundred and fifty plagues.

רַבִּי עֲקִיבָא אוֹמֵר: מִנַּיִן שֶׁכָּל מַכָּה וּמַכָּה, שֶׁהֵבִיא הַקָּדוֹשׁ בָּרוּךְ הוּא עַל הַמִּצְרִים בְּמִצְרַיִם, הָיְתָה שֶׁל חָמֵשׁ מַכּוֹת? שֶׁנֶּאֱמַר: יְשַׁלַּח בָּם חֲרוֹן אַפּוֹ, עֶבְרָה, וָזַעַם, וְצָרָה, מִשְׁלַחַת מַלְאֲכֵי רָעִים. חֲרוֹן אַפּוֹ אַחַת, עֶבְרָה שְׁתַּיִם, וָזַעַם שָׁלֹשׁ, וְצָרָה אַרְבַּע, מִשְׁלַחַת מַלְאֲכֵי רָעִים חָמֵשׁ. אֱמוֹר מֵעַתָּה: בְּמִצְרַיִם לָקוּ חֲמִשִּׁים מַכּוֹת, וְעַל הַיָּם לָקוּ חֲמִשִּׁים וּמָאתַיִם מַכּוֹת.

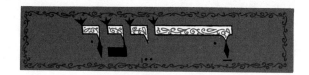

DAYYENU

DAYYENU is a rising crescendo of thanksgiving, beginning with gratitude for physical deliverance, and ending with gratitude for the spiritual blessings of the Sabbath and the Torah. Freedom is not enough. The Exodus must lead to Sinai. "Only he is truly free who studies and lives by the Torah." Freedom under law is necessary for security and happiness. The fifteen divine favors enumerated in this hymn are referred to as MAALOT and are said to correspond to the fifteen psalms which begin with the caption, "SHIR HAMAALOT." These psalms are said to have been sung by the Levites as they ascended the fifteen steps leading to the Sanctuary. Fifteen in Hebrew is YOD HEH, which designates the name of God.

DAYYENU has been variously translated as "it would have sufficed," "we should have been content," "for that alone we should have been grateful," and "we would have thought it enough." We shall leave the word DAYYENU untranslated.

Now let us join in singing this delightful hymn of thanksgiving.

How thankful we should be to God **For His many deeds of kindness to us!**	כַּמָּה מַעֲלוֹת טוֹבוֹת לַמָּקוֹם עָלֵינוּ !
Had God freed us from the Egyptians, **And not wrought judgment upon them,** DAYYENU.	אִלּוּ הוֹצִיאָנוּ מִמִּצְרַיִם, וְלֹא עָשָׂה בָהֶם שְׁפָטִים, דַּיֵּנוּ.
Had He wrought judgment upon the Egyptians, **And not destroyed their gods,** DAYYENU.	אִלּוּ עָשָׂה בָהֶם שְׁפָטִים, וְלֹא עָשָׂה בֵאלֹהֵיהֶם, דַּיֵּנוּ.
Had He destroyed their gods, **And not smitten their first-born,** DAYYENU.	אִלּוּ עָשָׂה בֵאלֹהֵיהֶם, וְלֹא הָרַג אֶת בְּכוֹרֵיהֶם, דַּיֵּנוּ.
Had He smitten their first-born, **And not given us their treasure,** DAYYENU.	אִלּוּ הָרַג אֶת בְּכוֹרֵיהֶם, וְלֹא נָתַן לָנוּ אֶת מָמוֹנָם, דַּיֵּנוּ.

23

Had He given us their treasure,
And not divided the Red Sea for us,

      DAYYENU.

אִלּוּ נָתַן לָנוּ אֶת מָמוֹנָם,
וְלֹא קָרַע לָנוּ אֶת הַיָּם,
דַּיֵּנוּ.

Had He divided the Red Sea for us,
And not let us pass through it dry-shod,

      DAYYENU.

אִלּוּ קָרַע לָנוּ אֶת הַיָּם,
וְלֹא הֶעֱבִירָנוּ בְתוֹכוֹ בֶּחָרָבָה,
דַּיֵּנוּ.

Had He let us pass through it dry-shod,
And not drowned our oppressors in it,

      DAYYENU.

אִלּוּ הֶעֱבִירָנוּ בְתוֹכוֹ בֶּחָרָבָה,
וְלֹא שִׁקַּע צָרֵינוּ בְּתוֹכוֹ,
דַּיֵּנוּ.

Had He drowned our oppressors in it,
And not sustained us in the wilderness for forty years,

      DAYYENU.

אִלּוּ שִׁקַּע צָרֵינוּ בְּתוֹכוֹ,
וְלֹא סִפֵּק צָרְכֵּנוּ בַּמִּדְבָּר
אַרְבָּעִים שָׁנָה,
דַּיֵּנוּ.

Had He sustained us in the wilderness for forty years,
And not fed us with manna,

      DAYYENU.

אִלּוּ סִפֵּק צָרְכֵּנוּ בַּמִּדְבָּר
אַרְבָּעִים שָׁנָה,
וְלֹא הֶאֱכִילָנוּ אֶת הַמָּן,
דַּיֵּנוּ.

Had He fed us with manna,
And not given us the Sabbath,

      DAYYENU.

אִלּוּ הֶאֱכִילָנוּ אֶת הַמָּן,
וְלֹא נָתַן לָנוּ אֶת הַשַּׁבָּת,
דַּיֵּנוּ.

Had He given us the Sabbath,
And not brought us to Mount Sinai,

      DAYYENU.

אִלּוּ נָתַן לָנוּ אֶת הַשַּׁבָּת,
וְלֹא קֵרְבָנוּ לִפְנֵי הַר סִינַי,
דַּיֵּנוּ.

Had He brought us to Mount Sinai,
And not given us the Torah,

      DAYYENU.

אִלּוּ קֵרְבָנוּ לִפְנֵי הַר סִינַי,
וְלֹא נָתַן לָנוּ אֶת הַתּוֹרָה,
דַּיֵּנוּ.

Had He given us the Torah,
And not brought us into the Land
    of Israel,
          DAYYENU.

אִלּוּ נָתַן לָנוּ אֶת הַתּוֹרָה,
וְלֹא הִכְנִיסָנוּ לְאֶרֶץ יִשְׂרָאֵל,
דַּיֵּנוּ.

Had He brought us into the Land
    of Israel,
And not built the Temple for us,
          DAYYENU.

אִלּוּ הִכְנִיסָנוּ לְאֶרֶץ יִשְׂרָאֵל,
וְלֹא בָנָה לָנוּ אֶת בֵּית הַבְּחִירָה,
דַּיֵּנוּ.

How manifold are God's blessings in double and redoubled measure! He freed us from the Egyptians and brought judgment upon them; He destroyed their gods and smote their first-born; He gave us their treasure and divided the Red Sea for us; He led us through it dry-shod, and drowned our oppressors in it; He sustained us in the wilderness for forty years and fed us with manna; He gave us the Sabbath and brought us to Mount Sinai; He gave us the Torah and brought us into the Land of Israel; He built for us the Temple where we prayed for the atonement of our sins.

עַל אַחַת כַּמָּה וְכַמָּה, טוֹבָה כְפוּלָה וּמְכֻפֶּלֶת לַמָּקוֹם עָלֵינוּ: שֶׁהוֹצִיאָנוּ מִמִּצְרַיִם, וְעָשָׂה בָהֶם שְׁפָטִים, וְעָשָׂה בֵאלֹהֵיהֶם, וְהָרַג אֶת בְּכוֹרֵיהֶם, וְנָתַן לָנוּ אֶת מָמוֹנָם, וְקָרַע לָנוּ אֶת הַיָּם, וְהֶעֱבִירָנוּ בְתוֹכוֹ בֶּחָרָבָה, וְשִׁקַּע צָרֵינוּ בְּתוֹכוֹ, וְסִפֵּק צָרְכֵּנוּ בַּמִּדְבָּר אַרְבָּעִים שָׁנָה, וְהֶאֱכִילָנוּ אֶת הַמָּן, וְנָתַן לָנוּ אֶת הַשַּׁבָּת, וְקֵרְבָנוּ לִפְנֵי הַר סִינַי, וְנָתַן לָנוּ אֶת הַתּוֹרָה, וְהִכְנִיסָנוּ לְאֶרֶץ יִשְׂרָאֵל, וּבָנָה לָנוּ אֶת בֵּית הַבְּחִירָה לְכַפֵּר עַל כָּל עֲוֹנוֹתֵינוּ.

Rabbi Gamaliel (grandson of the great Sage Hillel) said: "He who has not explained the following symbols of the Seder has not fulfilled his duty:

רַבָּן גַּמְלִיאֵל הָיָה אוֹמֵר: כָּל שֶׁלֹּא אָמַר שְׁלֹשָׁה דְבָרִים אֵלּוּ בַּפֶּסַח לֹא יָצָא יְדֵי חוֹבָתוֹ, וְאֵלּוּ הֵן:

Pesaḥ,   the Paschal Lamb;   פֶּסַח,

Matzah, the Unleavened Bread;   מַצָּה,

Maror,   the Bitter Herb.   וּמָרוֹר.

The following explanation of PESAḤ, MATZAH and MAROR is taken from the MISHNAH PESAḤIM 10:5.

One of the participants asks:

What is the meaning of the PASCHAL LAMB which our forefathers used to eat at the time when the Temple was still in existence?

פֶּסַח, שֶׁהָיוּ אֲבוֹתֵינוּ אוֹכְלִים בִּזְמַן שֶׁבֵּית הַמִּקְדָּשׁ הָיָה קַיָּם, עַל שׁוּם מָה?

The Leader points to the shank bone of the lamb and answers:

The PASCHAL LAMB is to remind us that the Holy One, praised be He, passed over the houses of our forefathers in Egypt, as it is written in the Bible: "You shall say that it is the sacrifice of the Lord's passover, for He passed over the houses of the Children of Israel in Egypt when He smote the Egyptians, but spared our houses. The people bowed their heads and worshiped." (Ex. 12:27)

עַל שׁוּם שֶׁפָּסַח הַקָּדוֹשׁ בָּרוּךְ הוּא עַל בָּתֵּי אֲבוֹתֵינוּ בְּמִצְרַיִם, שֶׁנֶּאֱמַר: וַאֲמַרְתֶּם זֶבַח פֶּסַח הוּא לַיְיָ, אֲשֶׁר פָּסַח עַל בָּתֵּי בְנֵי יִשְׂרָאֵל בְּמִצְרַיִם, בְּנָגְפּוֹ אֶת מִצְרַיִם וְאֶת בָּתֵּינוּ הִצִּיל; וַיִּקֹּד הָעָם וַיִּשְׁתַּחֲווּ.

Scholars maintain that, because the Egyptians worshiped the lamb, that animal was deliberately chosen to be sacrificed for Passover, to emphasize the fact that the Israelites rejected the worship of animals. Before the destruction of the Temple, a lamb, offered as a sacrifice, was roasted and eaten at the Seder. Later, when animal sacrifices were abolished, other meat was substituted. However, the meat served at the Seder was not to be roasted on an open flame because the lamb of the Paschal sacrifice had been roasted.

It is significant that the first ordinance of the Jewish religion concerns a family festival to celebrate the birth of freedom. "They shall take every man a lamb, according to their fathers' houses, a lamb for each household." (Ex. 12:13)

What an impressive sight it must have been when, from all parts of the land, people gathered in Jerusalem, and the head of each household brought a lamb to observe Passover with his family! Just as in the past, the Seder in our day is the family festival par excellence, for it brings together members of families and friends from near and far. May the Seder each year be a means of drawing us ever closer to our family and friends, and may it help to keep each Jewish home a miniature sanctuary where God's spirit shall dwell, and where reverence, love and peace shall prevail.

What is the meaning of the MATZAH that we eat?

מַצָּה זוֹ, שֶׁאָנוּ אוֹכְלִים,
עַל שׁוּם מָה?

The Leader raises the Matzah and answers:

The MATZAH is to remind us that before the dough which our forefathers prepared for bread had time to ferment, the supreme King of kings, the Holy One, praised be He, revealed Himself to them and redeemed them. We read in the Bible: "They baked matzah of the unleavened dough which they had brought out of Egypt, for it had not leavened because they were thrust out of Egypt and could not linger, nor had they prepared any food for the journey." (Ex. 12:39)

עַל שׁוּם שֶׁלֹּא הִסְפִּיק בְּצֵקָם שֶׁל
אֲבוֹתֵינוּ לְהַחֲמִיץ עַד שֶׁנִּגְלָה עֲלֵיהֶם
מֶלֶךְ מַלְכֵי הַמְּלָכִים, הַקָּדוֹשׁ בָּרוּךְ
הוּא, וּגְאָלָם, שֶׁנֶּאֱמַר: וַיֹּאפוּ אֶת
הַבָּצֵק אֲשֶׁר הוֹצִיאוּ מִמִּצְרַיִם, עֻגֹת
מַצּוֹת כִּי לֹא חָמֵץ; כִּי גֹרְשׁוּ מִמִּצְרַיִם,
וְלֹא יָכְלוּ לְהִתְמַהְמֵהַּ, וְגַם צֵדָה לֹא
עָשׂוּ לָהֶם.

Our Sages found an ethical significance in the command: "You shall observe the Feast of Matzot." (Ex. 12:17) By changing the vowels, the word MATZOT becomes MITZVOT. "You shall observe the MITZVOT" (commandments of the Torah). Good deeds and ritual are combined in Judaism. Just as one should not allow the matzah to sour due to any delay in baking, so one should not permit a mitzvah to sour by postponing its performance.

Leaven is the symbol of evil and selfishness. Just as we search and remove the leaven from the home, so should we search our hearts to rid ourselves of all that degrades and debases.

Since the enslavement of the Israelites preceded their emancipation, one would expect the explanation of the MAROR, the symbol of bondage, to precede the explanation of the MATZAH, which reminds us of freedom. The reverse is the case, as if to indicate that there may be a tendency on the part of the enslaved supinely to accept their condition of servitude and do nothing about it. One who has always been a slave does not understand freedom or its privileges and responsibilities. That is why the explanation of the matzah, a reminder of freedom, is first emphasized. Only those who have experienced freedom can know the bitterness of oppression. It is therefore the duty of those who have attained freedom to work unceasingly for the liberation of all who are still oppressed.

What is the meaning of the BITTER HERBS which we eat?

רוֹר זֶה, שֶׁאָנוּ אוֹכְלִים, עַל שׁוּם מָה?

The Leader points to the Maror *and answers:*

The MAROR is to remind us that the Egyptians embittered the lives of our forefathers in Egypt, as the Bible explains: "They made their lives bitter with hard labor, with mortar and brick, and with every kind of work in the field. All the labor which the Egyptians forced upon them was harsh." (Ex. 1:14)

עַל שׁוּם שֶׁמֵּרְרוּ הַמִּצְרִים אֶת חַיֵּי אֲבוֹתֵינוּ בְּמִצְרַיִם, שֶׁנֶּאֱמַר: וַיְמָרְרוּ אֶת חַיֵּיהֶם בַּעֲבֹדָה קָשָׁה, בְּחֹמֶר וּבִלְבֵנִים, וּבְכָל עֲבֹדָה בַּשָּׂדֶה; אֵת כָּל עֲבֹדָתָם אֲשֶׁר עָבְדוּ בָהֶם בְּפָרֶךְ.

The following passage emphasizes our strong bond with Jewish history, its unity and continuity. In every age, Pharaohs have arisen to oppress our people. The hurt of any Jew anywhere became the hurt of all Jews everywhere. We therefore feel that when our people were slaves in Egypt, it is as though we also were slaves; when they were redeemed, we were redeemed. And now even though we are free men in a free land, we hear the cries of our brothers and all others who are enslaved. We know that our responsibility shall not cease until all who groan under the yoke of tyranny shall be emancipated.

IN every generation each Jew should regard himself as though he personally went forth from Egypt. That is what the Bible means when it says: "And you shall tell your son on that day, saying, 'It is because of what the Lord did for *me* when I went forth from Egypt.'" (Ex. 13:8) It was not only our forefathers whom the Holy One, praised be He, redeemed from slavery, but us also did He redeem together with them, as we read: "He brought *us* out from there so that He might bring us into the land, and give us this land which He promised to our forefathers." (Deut. 6:23)

כָּל דּוֹר וָדוֹר חַיָּב אָדָם לִרְאוֹת אֶת עַצְמוֹ כְּאִלּוּ הוּא יָצָא מִמִּצְרַיִם, שֶׁנֶּאֱמַר: וְהִגַּדְתָּ לְבִנְךָ בַּיּוֹם הַהוּא לֵאמֹר: בַּעֲבוּר זֶה עָשָׂה יְיָ לִי בְּצֵאתִי מִמִּצְרַיִם. לֹא אֶת אֲבוֹתֵינוּ בִּלְבָד גָּאַל הַקָּדוֹשׁ בָּרוּךְ הוּא, אֶלָּא אַף אוֹתָנוּ גָּאַל עִמָּהֶם, שֶׁנֶּאֱמַר: וְאוֹתָנוּ הוֹצִיא מִשָּׁם, לְמַעַן הָבִיא אֹתָנוּ, לָתֶת לָנוּ אֶת הָאָרֶץ אֲשֶׁר נִשְׁבַּע לַאֲבֹתֵינוּ.

28

In gratitude for all the miracles which God has performed for our fathers and for us from the days of old to this time, we raise our cups of wine and together say:

herefore, we should thank and praise, laud and glorify, exalt and honor, extol and adore God who performed all these miracles for our fathers and for us. He brought us from slavery to freedom, from sorrow to joy, from mourning to festivity, from darkness to great light, and from bondage to redemption. Let us, then, sing unto Him a new song: Halleluyah, praise the Lord!

לְפִיכָךְ אֲנַחְנוּ חַיָּבִים לְהוֹדוֹת, לְהַלֵּל, לְשַׁבֵּחַ, לְפָאֵר, לְרוֹמֵם, לְהַדֵּר, לְבָרֵךְ, לְעַלֵּה וּלְקַלֵּס לְמִי שֶׁעָשָׂה לַאֲבוֹתֵינוּ וְלָנוּ אֶת כָּל הַנִּסִּים הָאֵלּוּ. הוֹצִיאָנוּ מֵעַבְדוּת לְחֵרוּת, מִיָּגוֹן לְשִׂמְחָה, מֵאֵבֶל לְיוֹם טוֹב, וּמֵאֲפֵלָה לְאוֹר גָּדוֹל, וּמִשִּׁעְבּוּד לִגְאֻלָּה. וְנֹאמַר לְפָנָיו שִׁירָה חֲדָשָׁה; הַלְלוּיָהּ !

The wine cups are set down.

HALLEL

The following psalms in the Hallel are the same as those the Levites chanted in the Temple when the Paschal sacrifices were offered. Note the expression, "servants of the Lord." Our Sages explain: "Heretofore you were servants of Pharaoh; now you are servants of the Lord. You are My servants, and servants cannot possess other servants." (Talmud, Meg. 14a)

GOD CARES FOR THE LOWLY

Responsive Reading

PSALM 113

Halleluyah!

O servants of the Lord,

Praise the name of the Lord.

Praised be the name of the Lord
From this time forth and
forever.

From the rising of the sun unto
its setting,

The Lord's name is to be praised.

תהלים קיג

הַלְלוּיָהּ !

הַלְלוּ, עַבְדֵי יְיָ,

הַלְלוּ אֶת שֵׁם יְיָ.

יְהִי שֵׁם יְיָ מְבֹרָךְ,

מֵעַתָּה וְעַד עוֹלָם.

מִמִּזְרַח שֶׁמֶשׁ עַד מְבוֹאוֹ,

מְהֻלָּל שֵׁם יְיָ.

The Lord is supreme above all nations; His glory is above the heavens.	רָם עַל כָּל גּוֹיִם יְיָ, עַל הַשָּׁמַיִם כְּבוֹדוֹ.
Who is like the Lord our God, Enthroned so high,	מִי כַּיְיָ אֱלֹהֵינוּ, הַמַּגְבִּיהִי לָשָׁבֶת.
Yet who looks down, To consider both heaven and earth?	הַמַּשְׁפִּילִי לִרְאוֹת בַּשָּׁמַיִם וּבָאָרֶץ?
He raises up the poor out of the dust, And lifts up the needy from the pit,	מְקִימִי מֵעָפָר דָּל, מֵאַשְׁפֹּת יָרִים אֶבְיוֹן.
To seat them together with princes, Together with the princes of his people.	לְהוֹשִׁיבִי עִם נְדִיבִים, עִם נְדִיבֵי עַמּוֹ.
He makes the childless wife A happy mother of children.	מוֹשִׁיבִי עֲקֶרֶת הַבַּיִת, אֵם הַבָּנִים שְׂמֵחָה;
Halleluyah!	הַלְלוּיָהּ !

WHEN ISRAEL WENT FORTH FROM EGYPT

Responsive Reading

PSALM 114	תהלים קיד
When Israel went forth from Egypt, The house of Jacob from a people strange of tongue,	בְּצֵאת יִשְׂרָאֵל מִמִּצְרָיִם, בֵּית יַעֲקֹב מֵעַם לֹעֵז.
Judah became God's Sanctuary, Israel, His own dominion.	הָיְתָה יְהוּדָה לְקָדְשׁוֹ, יִשְׂרָאֵל מַמְשְׁלוֹתָיו.
The sea saw it, and fled; The Jordan turned back in its course.	הַיָּם רָאָה וַיָּנָס; הַיַּרְדֵּן יִסֹּב לְאָחוֹר.
The mountains, affrighted, skipped like rams, The hills, like young lambs.	הֶהָרִים רָקְדוּ כְאֵילִים, גְּבָעוֹת כִּבְנֵי צֹאן.
What ails you, O sea, that you flee? O Jordan, that you turn back in your course?	מַה לְּךָ הַיָּם כִּי תָנוּס? הַיַּרְדֵּן, תִּסֹּב לְאָחוֹר?

30

You mountains, that you skip
like rams;
And you hills, like young
lambs?

Tremble, O earth, at the presence
of the Lord,
At the presence of the God of
Jacob,
Who turns the rock into a pool
of water,
The flinty rock into a flowing
fountain.

הֶהָרִים, תִּרְקְדוּ כְאֵילִים;
גְּבָעוֹת, כִּבְנֵי צֹאן?

מִלִּפְנֵי אָדוֹן חוּלִי אָרֶץ,
מִלִּפְנֵי אֱלוֹהַּ יַעֲקֹב.

הַהֹפְכִי הַצּוּר אֲגַם מָיִם,
חַלָּמִישׁ לְמַעְיְנוֹ מָיִם.

31

Rabbi Akiba is responsible for including in the following prayer the hope of a future redemption — the restoration of Zion. Thus in this prayer the masculine form, SHIR ḤADASH (a new song), denotes the deliverance that will take place in the future, whereas the feminine form SHIRAH ḤADASHAH, in the introduction to the Hallel (page 29), refers to the redemption from Egypt which has already taken place.

Participants raise their second cup of wine.

This cup is not full because we spilled off some of its content when we enumerated the plagues inflicted upon the Egyptians. By drinking from this partially filled cup, we express our sympathy for the Egyptians who lost their lives when Israel attained freedom.

Praised be Thou, O Lord our God, King of the universe, who redeemed us, and redeemed our fathers from Egypt, and enabled us to reach this night on which we eat MATZAH and MAROR. Even so, O Lord our God and God of our fathers, do Thou enable us to reach in peace other holy days and festivals when we may rejoice in the restoration of Zion, Thy city, and find delight in serving Thee. There we shall partake of the Paschal meal and bring Thee the offerings which shall be acceptable unto Thee. And there we shall sing unto Thee a new song of praise for our freedom and redemption. Praised be Thou, O Lord, Redeemer of Israel.

בָּרוּךְ אַתָּה, יְיָ אֱלֹהֵינוּ, מֶלֶךְ הָעוֹלָם, אֲשֶׁר גְּאָלָנוּ וְגָאַל אֶת אֲבוֹתֵינוּ מִמִּצְרַיִם, וְהִגִּיעָנוּ לַלַּיְלָה הַזֶּה, לֶאֱכָל בּוֹ מַצָּה וּמָרוֹר. כֵּן, יְיָ אֱלֹהֵינוּ וֵאלֹהֵי אֲבוֹתֵינוּ, יַגִּיעֵנוּ לְמוֹעֲדִים וְלִרְגָלִים אֲחֵרִים, הַבָּאִים לִקְרָאתֵנוּ לְשָׁלוֹם, שְׂמֵחִים בְּבִנְיַן עִירֶךָ, וְשָׂשִׂים בַּעֲבוֹדָתֶךָ. וְנֹאכַל שָׁם מִן הַזְּבָחִים וּמִן הַפְּסָחִים, אֲשֶׁר יַגִּיעַ דָּמָם עַל קִיר מִזְבַּחֲךָ לְרָצוֹן, וְנוֹדֶה לְךָ שִׁיר חָדָשׁ עַל גְּאֻלָּתֵנוּ וְעַל פְּדוּת נַפְשֵׁנוּ. בָּרוּךְ אַתָּה, יְיָ, גָּאַל יִשְׂרָאֵל.

After the blessing, drink this second cup of wine while reclining to the left.

בָּרוּךְ אַתָּה יְיָ אֱלֹהֵינוּ מֶלֶךְ הָעוֹלָם בּוֹרֵא פְּרִי הַגָּפֶן:

Baruḥ atta Adonai, elohenu meleḥ ha-olam, boray p'ri ha-gafen.

Praised be Thou, O Lord our God, King of the Universe, Creator of the Fruit of the Vine.

6. Raḥatz — Wash the Hands Before the Meal —

An example of combining hygiene and religion; an application of "Cleanliness is next to Godliness."

בָּרוּךְ אַתָּה, יְיָ אֱלֹהֵינוּ, מֶלֶךְ הָעוֹלָם, אֲשֶׁר קִדְּשָׁנוּ בְּמִצְוֹתָיו וְצִוָּנוּ עַל נְטִילַת יָדֵיִם.

Praised Be Thou, O Lord our God, King of the Universe, Who hast Sanctified Us with Thy Commandments and Enjoined upon Us the Mitzvah of Washing the Hands.

7. Motzi — Say the Ha-Motzi —

8. Matzah — Recite the Blessing for the Matzah —

A piece of the uppermost matzah and a piece of the broken middle matzah is distributed to each participant. After salting the two pieces of matzah, recite the usual HA-MOTZI blessing and then the special blessing for the matzah; then eat both pieces of matzah while reclining to the left.

בָּרוּךְ אַתָּה, יְיָ אֱלֹהֵינוּ, מֶלֶךְ הָעוֹלָם, הַמּוֹצִיא לֶחֶם מִן הָאָרֶץ.
Baruḥ atta Adonai, elohenu meleḥ ha-olam, hamotzi lehem min ha-aretz

בָּרוּךְ אַתָּה, יְיָ אֱלֹהֵינוּ, מֶלֶךְ הָעוֹלָם, אֲשֶׁר קִדְּשָׁנוּ בְּמִצְוֹתָיו וְצִוָּנוּ עַל אֲכִילַת מַצָּה.
Baruḥ atta Adonai, elohenu meleḥ ha-olam, asher kidshanu b'mitzvo-tav ve-tzivanu al aḥilat matza.

Praised be Thou, O Lord our God, King of the Universe, Who Bringest forth Sustenance from the Earth.

Praised be Thou, O Lord our God, King of the Universe, Who hast Sanctified Us with Thy Commandments and Enjoined upon Us the Mitzvah of Eating Unleavened Bread.

The matzah is salted as a reminder that all sacrifices brought into the Temple were salted before being burned on the altar.

We are obliged to eat matzah at the Seder only. We are not obliged to eat it at other times during the Passover festival, but we are to abstain from eating ḤAMETZ. Matzah, the bread of poverty, is also vested with an ethical significance. Leaven is the symbol of YETZER HARA, the evil impulse. Matzah, the symbol of purity, represents freedom derived from obedience to the YETZER HATOV, the good inclination.

9. Maror — Eat the Bitter Herbs —

The bitter herbs of which we shall partake, are a reminder of the bitterness the Israelites experienced in Egypt. The ḤAROSET into which the bitter herbs are dipped, symbolizes the mortar and bricks with which our forefathers were forced to construct cities and treasure-houses for Pharaoh.

Life is bitter-sweet. The sweet and pleasant taste of the ḤAROSET impresses upon us that, no matter how bitter and dark the present appears, we should hopefully look forward to better days. "Sweet are the uses of adversity." Since MAROR is a symbol of bondage, we do not recline while eating it.

A portion of the bitter herbs is dipped into the ḤAROSET *and eaten by each one present after reciting the following blessing:*

בָּרוּךְ אַתָּה, יְיָ אֱלֹהֵינוּ, מֶלֶךְ הָעוֹלָם, אֲשֶׁר קִדְּשָׁנוּ בְּמִצְוֹתָיו וְצִוָּנוּ עַל אֲכִילַת מָרוֹר.

Praised be Thou, O Lord our God, King of the Universe, Who hast Sanctified Us by Thy Commandments and Enjoined upon Us the Mitzvah of Eating the Bitter Herbs.

10. Korekh – Eat the Matzah and Maror Sandwich —

(Called "Hillel's Sandwich")*

The bottom matzah is broken into small pieces. Each person receives two pieces between which are placed some of the bitter herbs.

To the Sage Hillel, eating MATZAH and MAROR together was not a trivial matter. To him, slavery and freedom were merged in one historical event. The bread of poverty became the bread of freedom and should be tasted together with the bitter MAROR, so that one should know the bitterness of slavery and the joy of freedom. In time of freedom, we must not forget the bitterness of slavery; in time of oppression, we must keep alive the hope of freedom. That is why Hillel's practice of eating MATZAH and MAROR together has such an important message for us today.

* The Sage Hillel, and not the Earl of Sandwich, the employer of Samuel Pepys, was the originator of the sandwich.

It was the Sage Hillel who, two thousand years ago, explained the essence of Judaism: "What is hateful to you, do not do to your fellow man. This is the whole Torah; the rest is the commentary thereof. Go and learn it." (Shab. 31a)

In unison

זֵכֶר לְמִקְדָּשׁ כְּהִלֵּל.

As a reminder of the Temple, we follow the practice of Hillel.

While the Temple was still in existence, Hillel would eat together in a sandwich some MATZAH and MAROR, to fulfill the Biblical command: "They shall eat it (the Paschal Lamb) together with unleavened bread and bitter herbs." (Num. 9:11)

כֵּן עָשָׂה הִלֵּל בִּזְמַן שֶׁבֵּית הַמִּקְדָּשׁ הָיָה קַיָם: הָיָה כּוֹרֵךְ (פֶּסַח) מַצָּה וּמָרוֹר וְאוֹכֵל בְּיַחַד, לְקַיֵם מַה שֶׁנֶּאֱמַר: עַל מַצּוֹת וּמְרֹרִים יֹאכְלֻהוּ.

All eat the sandwich.

11. Shulḥan Orekh —

ENJOY THE FESTIVAL MEAL —

Now that we have completed the first part of the Haggadah, we are ready for the Passover meal. When the Temple was in existence, roasted lamb was eaten at the Seder. Since the destruction of the Temple, lamb is not served, and nothing is included in the meal that has been roasted on an open flame.

Remove the ritual symbols from the table.

In many homes, it is customary to begin the meal with a hard-boiled egg usually dipped in salt water. Three interesting explanations are given for this practice. First, unlike most foods which become softer, the more it is boiled, the harder the egg becomes. This indicates the stubborn resistance of the Jews to those who sought to crush them. Secondly, the egg is regarded as the symbol of new life; a chick must break its egg to emerge into life. Finally, since the roasted egg on the Seder plate is a reminder of the sacifice that took place in the Temple of old, we eat the egg to remind us of the destruction of the Temple and of our obligation to aid in the rebuilding of Zion today.*

---

* It is interesting to note that the first day of Passover always falls on the same day of the week as TISHAH B'AV, the ninth day of the month of AV, which commemorates the destruction of the first Temple by the Babylonians in 586 B. C. E., and the destruction of the second Temple by the Romans in 70 C. E.

12. Tzafun — EAT THE AFIKOMAN —

Since the meal cannot be ritually completed without eating the AFIKOMAN, the Leader or Host now calls for the AFIKOMAN (the portion of the middle matzah that was hidden). The child who finds it receives a reward. The AFIKOMAN is our substitute for the Paschal Lamb, which in days of old, was the final food of the Seder feast. Each person is given a portion, which is eaten in a reclining position.

Fill the third cup of wine.

13. Barekh —
RECITE THE BIRKAT HAMAZON (BLESSING AFTER THE MEAL) —

It is appropriate to introduce the BIRKAT HAMAZON with the singing of Psalm 126, which describes the great joy of the exiles twenty-five hundred years ago, when they returned from Babylonia to Zion. Throughout the ages, this same psalm brought hope to the Jews that Zion would be restored and provide a homeland for the homeless and oppressed of their people.

SHIR HA-MAALOT — THE RETURN TO ZION

Shir ha-ma-a-lot.
B'shuv Adonai et shivat tziyon
ha-yeenu k'holmim.
Az yimalay s'hok peenu,
u-l'sho-naynu rina;
az yomru va-goyim,
higdil Adonai la-asot im ayleh.
Higdil Adonai la-asot imanu,
ha-yeenu s'mayhim.
Shuva Adonai et sh'vitaynu,
ka-a-fikim ba-negev.
Ha-zoreem b'dima, b'rina yiktzoru.
Haloh yaylayh u-vaho,
nosay me-sheh ha-zara;
bo yavo v'rina nosay alumotav.

שִׁיר הַמַּעֲלוֹת.

בְּשׁוּב יְיָ אֶת שִׁיבַת צִיּוֹן

הָיִינוּ כְּחֹלְמִים.

אָז יִמָּלֵא שְׂחוֹק פִּינוּ,

וּלְשׁוֹנֵנוּ רִנָּה;

אָז יֹאמְרוּ בַגּוֹיִם,

הִגְדִּיל יְיָ לַעֲשׂוֹת עִם אֵלֶּה.

הִגְדִּיל יְיָ לַעֲשׂוֹת עִמָּנוּ,

הָיִינוּ שְׂמֵחִים.

שׁוּבָה יְיָ אֶת שְׁבִיתֵנוּ,

כַּאֲפִיקִים בַּנֶּגֶב.

הַזֹּרְעִים בְּדִמְעָה, בְּרִנָּה יִקְצֹרוּ.

הָלוֹךְ יֵלֵךְ וּבָכֹה נֹשֵׂא מֶשֶׁךְ הַזָּרַע;

בֹּא יָבֹא בְרִנָּה נֹשֵׂא אֲלֻמֹּתָיו.

When the Lord brought the exiles back to Zion, we were as in a dream. Then was our mouth filled with laughter, and our tongue with joyous song. Then it was told among the nations: "The Lord has done great things for them." Yea, the Lord has done great things for us, and we are rejoiced. O Lord, bring back our exiles, like streams in the desert. They who sow in tears shall reap in joy. Though he weeps as he scatters his measure of seed, he shall return with joyous song as he carries home his sheaves.

When three or more have eaten together, the following introduction to the BIRKAT HAMAZON *(Blessing after the Meal) is added:*

(When ten or more are present, include the words in brackets.)

Leader

Let us say the blessing for our food.   .רַבּוֹתַי, נְבָרֵךְ

Participants, and then Leader

Praised be the name of the Lord from this time forth and forever.   .יְהִי שֵׁם יְיָ מְבֹרָךְ מֵעַתָּה וְעַד עוֹלָם

Leader

With the permission of those present, let us praise Him [our God] of whose bounty we have partaken.   בִּרְשׁוּת מָרָנָן וְרַבּוֹתַי נְבָרֵךְ [אֱלֹהֵינוּ] שֶׁאָכַלְנוּ מִשֶּׁלּוֹ.

Participants, then Leader

Praised be He [our God] of whose bounty we have partaken and through whose goodness we live.   בָּרוּךְ [אֱלֹהֵינוּ] שֶׁאָכַלְנוּ מִשֶּׁלּוֹ וּבְטוּבוֹ חָיִינוּ.

All

Praised be He and praised be His name.   .בָּרוּךְ הוּא וּבָרוּךְ שְׁמוֹ

Baruḥ atta Adonai, eloheynu meleḥ ha-olam, ha-zan et ha-olam ku-lo b'tu-vo, b'ḥen b'ḥesed u-v'raḥamim. Hu noten leḥem l'ḥol basar kee l'olam ḥasdo. U-v'tuvo hagadol tamid lo ḥasar lanu, V'al yeḥsar lanu ma-zone l'olam va-ed, ba-avur Sh'mo ha-gadol. Kee hu el zan u-m'farnes la-kol, u-maytiv la-kol, u-mayḥin ma-zone l'ḥol briyotav asher ba-ra. Baruḥ atta Adonai ha-zan et ha-kol.

(Praised be God who by His grace sustains the word. May we never lack sustenance. Praised be God who provides food for all.)

רוּךְ אַתָּה, יְיָ אֱלֹהֵינוּ, מֶלֶךְ הָעוֹלָם, הַזָּן אֶת הָעוֹלָם כֻּלּוֹ בְּטוּבוֹ, בְּחֵן בְּחֶסֶד וּבְרַחֲמִים. הוּא נוֹתֵן לֶחֶם לְכָל בָּשָׂר, כִּי לְעוֹלָם חַסְדּוֹ. וּבְטוּבוֹ הַגָּדוֹל תָּמִיד לֹא חָסַר לָנוּ, וְאַל יֶחְסַר לָנוּ מָזוֹן לְעוֹלָם וָעֶד בַּעֲבוּר שְׁמוֹ הַגָּדוֹל. כִּי הוּא אֵל זָן וּמְפַרְנֵס לַכֹּל, וּמֵטִיב לַכֹּל, וּמֵכִין מָזוֹן לְכָל בְּרִיּוֹתָיו אֲשֶׁר בָּרָא. בָּרוּךְ אַתָּה, יְיָ, הַזָּן אֶת הַכֹּל.

37

We thank Thee, O Lord our God, for the good, pleasant, and spacious land which Thou hast given as an inheritance to our fathers, for having liberated us from the land of Egypt, and redeemed us from the house of bondage. We thank Thee for Thy covenant sealed in our flesh, for Thy Torah which Thou hast taught us, and for Thy laws which Thou hast made known to us. We also thank Thee for the gift of life which Thou, in Thy grace and lovingkindness, hast bestowed upon us, and for the sustenance with which Thou dost nourish and maintain us continually, in every season, every day, even every hour.

For all these blessings, O Lord our God, we give Thee thanks and we praise Thee. May Thy name be praised by every living being continually and forever, as we are told in the Torah: "When you have eaten and are satisfied, you shall praise the Lord your God for the good land which He has given you." (Deut. 8:10) Praised be Thou, O Lord, for the land and its produce.

O Lord our God, remember in mercy, Israel Thy people, Jerusalem Thy city, Zion the abode of Thy glory, the royal house of David, Thine anointed, and the great and holy Temple called by Thy name. Our God and Father, tend and nourish us, sustain and maintain us, and speedily grant us surcease from all our sorrows.

נוֹדֶה לְּךָ, יְיָ אֱלֹהֵינוּ, עַל שֶׁהִנְחַלְתָּ לַאֲבוֹתֵינוּ אֶרֶץ חֶמְדָּה טוֹבָה וּרְחָבָה; וְעַל שֶׁהוֹצֵאתָנוּ, יְיָ אֱלֹהֵינוּ, מֵאֶרֶץ מִצְרַיִם, וּפְדִיתָנוּ מִבֵּית עֲבָדִים; וְעַל בְּרִיתְךָ שֶׁחָתַמְתָּ בִּבְשָׂרֵנוּ; וְעַל תּוֹרָתְךָ שֶׁלִּמַּדְתָּנוּ; וְעַל חֻקֶּיךָ שֶׁהוֹדַעְתָּנוּ; וְעַל חַיִּים, חֵן וָחֶסֶד שֶׁחוֹנַנְתָּנוּ; וְעַל אֲכִילַת מָזוֹן שָׁאַתָּה זָן וּמְפַרְנֵס אוֹתָנוּ תָּמִיד, בְּכָל יוֹם וּבְכָל עֵת וּבְכָל שָׁעָה.

וְעַל הַכֹּל, יְיָ אֱלֹהֵינוּ, אֲנַחְנוּ מוֹדִים לָךְ, וּמְבָרְכִים אוֹתָךְ; יִתְבָּרַךְ שִׁמְךָ בְּפִי כָל חַי תָּמִיד לְעוֹלָם וָעֶד, כַּכָּתוּב: וְאָכַלְתָּ וְשָׂבָעְתָּ, וּבֵרַכְתָּ אֶת יְיָ אֱלֹהֶיךָ עַל הָאָרֶץ הַטֹּבָה אֲשֶׁר נָתַן לָךְ. בָּרוּךְ אַתָּה, יְיָ, עַל הָאָרֶץ וְעַל הַמָּזוֹן.

רַחֵם, יְיָ אֱלֹהֵינוּ, עַל יִשְׂרָאֵל עַמֶּךָ, וְעַל יְרוּשָׁלַיִם עִירֶךָ, וְעַל צִיּוֹן מִשְׁכַּן כְּבוֹדֶךָ, וְעַל מַלְכוּת בֵּית דָּוִד מְשִׁיחֶךָ, וְעַל הַבַּיִת הַגָּדוֹל וְהַקָּדוֹשׁ שֶׁנִּקְרָא שִׁמְךָ עָלָיו. אֱלֹהֵינוּ, אָבִינוּ, רְעֵנוּ, זוּנֵנוּ, פַּרְנְסֵנוּ וְכַלְכְּלֵנוּ וְהַרְוִיחֵנוּ; וְהַרְוַח לָנוּ, יְיָ אֱלֹהֵינוּ, מְהֵרָה מִכָּל צָרוֹתֵינוּ. וְנָא, אַל

O Lord our God, let us not be dependent upon the alms of our fellow men or their favors, but rather let us look to Thy hand that is full, open and generous, so that we may never be humiliated or put to shame.

תַּצְרִיכֵנוּ, יְיָ אֱלֹהֵינוּ, לֹא לִידֵי מַתְּנַת בָּשָׂר וָדָם וְלֹא לִידֵי הַלְוָאָתָם, כִּי אִם לְיָדְךָ הַמְּלֵאָה הַפְּתוּחָה, הַקְּדוֹשָׁה וְהָרְחָבָה, שֶׁלֹּא נֵבוֹשׁ וְלֹא נִכָּלֵם לְעוֹלָם וָעֶד.

On Sabbath add:

O Lord our God, strengthen us by Thy commandments, and especially by the commandment concerning the seventh day, this great and holy Sabbath. This day is great and holy before Thee, for in Thy love Thou hast decreed that we cease from all labor and rest thereon. O Lord our God, may it be Thy will to grant us such repose that no trouble, sorrow or anguish shall disturb our day of rest. May we behold Zion comforted, and Jerusalem, Thy holy city, rebuilt, for Thou art the Lord of redemption and of consolation.

רְצֵה וְהַחֲלִיצֵנוּ, יְיָ אֱלֹהֵינוּ בְּמִצְוֹתֶיךָ וּבְמִצְוַת יוֹם הַשְּׁבִיעִי, הַשַּׁבָּת הַגָּדוֹל וְהַקָּדוֹשׁ הַזֶּה; כִּי יוֹם זֶה גָּדוֹל וְקָדוֹשׁ הוּא לְפָנֶיךָ, לִשְׁבָּת בּוֹ וְלָנוּחַ בּוֹ בְּאַהֲבָה כְּמִצְוַת רְצוֹנֶךָ. וּבִרְצוֹנְךָ הָנַח לָנוּ, יְיָ אֱלֹהֵינוּ, שֶׁלֹּא תְהֵא צָרָה, וְיָגוֹן וַאֲנָחָה, בְּיוֹם מְנוּחָתֵנוּ. וְהַרְאֵנוּ, יְיָ אֱלֹהֵינוּ, בְּנֶחָמַת צִיּוֹן עִירֶךָ, וּבְבִנְיַן יְרוּשָׁלַיִם עִיר קָדְשֶׁךָ, כִּי אַתָּה הוּא בַּעַל הַיְשׁוּעוֹת וּבַעַל הַנֶּחָמוֹת.

Our God and God of our fathers, on this Festival of Unleavened Bread, mayest Thou be mindful of us and our fathers. Hasten the Messianic era; remember Jerusalem, Thy holy city, and all Thy people, the house of Israel, for deliverance, grace, lovingkindness, mercy, life and peace. Remember us this day, O Lord our God, to bless us with life and wellbeing. With Thy promise of deliverance and mercy, spare us and be gracious unto us, have compassion upon us and save us. We look to Thee, O our God, for Thou art a gracious and merciful King.

אֱלֹהֵינוּ וֵאלֹהֵי אֲבוֹתֵינוּ, יַעֲלֶה וְיָבֹא, וְיַגִּיעַ וְיֵרָאֶה, וְיֵרָצֶה וְיִשָּׁמַע, וְיִפָּקֵד וְיִזָּכֵר זִכְרוֹנֵנוּ וּפִקְדוֹנֵנוּ, וְזִכְרוֹן אֲבוֹתֵינוּ, וְזִכְרוֹן מָשִׁיחַ בֶּן דָּוִד עַבְדֶּךָ, וְזִכְרוֹן יְרוּשָׁלַיִם עִיר קָדְשֶׁךָ, וְזִכְרוֹן כָּל עַמְּךָ בֵּית יִשְׂרָאֵל לְפָנֶיךָ, לִפְלֵיטָה וּלְטוֹבָה, לְחֵן וּלְחֶסֶד וּלְרַחֲמִים, לְחַיִּים וּלְשָׁלוֹם, בְּיוֹם חַג הַמַּצּוֹת הַזֶּה. זָכְרֵנוּ, יְיָ אֱלֹהֵינוּ, בּוֹ לְטוֹבָה וּפָקְדֵנוּ בּוֹ לִבְרָכָה, וְהוֹשִׁיעֵנוּ בּוֹ לְחַיִּים. וּבִדְבַר יְשׁוּעָה וְרַחֲמִים חוּס וְחָנֵּנוּ, וְרַחֵם עָלֵינוּ וְהוֹשִׁיעֵנוּ כִּי אֵלֶיךָ עֵינֵינוּ, כִּי אֵל מֶלֶךְ חַנּוּן וְרַחוּם אָתָּה.

39

ebuild Jerusalem, Thy holy city, speedily in our lifetime. Praised be Thou, O Lord, who in Thy mercy rebuildest Jerusalem. Amen.

Praised be Thou, O Lord our God, King of the universe. Thou art God, our Father, our Sovereign, our Mighty One, our Creator, our Redeemer, our Maker. O Holy One of Jacob, Thou art also our Holy One. O Shepherd of Israel, Thou art also our Shepherd. Thou art the good King who doest good to all. Thou who hast shown us kindness day by day and art good to us, mayest Thou continue Thy goodness to us. As Thou hast ever bestowed Thy bounties upon us, mayest Thou continue to bless us with Thy grace, lovingkindness, compassion and deliverance, prosperity, redemption and consolation, sustenance and mercy, a life of peace and all that is good. Mayest Thou never withhold Thy goodness from us.

May the merciful Father reign over us for ever and ever.

May the merciful Father be extolled in heaven and on earth.

May the merciful Father be praised in all generations; may He be glorified through us to all eternity; may He be honored among us forever.

May the merciful Father grant us an honorable livelihood.

וּבְנֵה יְרוּשָׁלַיִם עִיר הַקֹּדֶשׁ בִּמְהֵרָה בְיָמֵינוּ. בָּרוּךְ אַתָּה, יְיָ, בּוֹנֵה בְרַחֲמָיו יְרוּשָׁלָיִם, אָמֵן.

בָּרוּךְ אַתָּה, יְיָ אֱלֹהֵינוּ, מֶלֶךְ הָעוֹלָם, הָאֵל, אָבִינוּ, מַלְכֵּנוּ, אַדִּירֵנוּ, בּוֹרְאֵנוּ, גּוֹאֲלֵנוּ, יוֹצְרֵנוּ, קְדוֹשֵׁנוּ, קְדוֹשׁ יַעֲקֹב, רוֹעֵנוּ, רוֹעֵה יִשְׂרָאֵל, הַמֶּלֶךְ הַטּוֹב וְהַמֵּטִיב לַכֹּל, שֶׁבְּכָל יוֹם וָיוֹם הוּא הֵטִיב, הוּא מֵטִיב, הוּא יֵיטִיב לָנוּ. הוּא גְמָלָנוּ, הוּא גוֹמְלֵנוּ, הוּא יִגְמְלֵנוּ לָעַד, לְחֵן וּלְחֶסֶד וּלְרַחֲמִים וּלְרֶוַח, הַצָּלָה וְהַצְלָחָה, בְּרָכָה וִישׁוּעָה, נֶחָמָה פַּרְנָסָה וְכַלְכָּלָה, וְרַחֲמִים וְחַיִּים וְשָׁלוֹם וְכָל טוֹב, וּמִכָּל טוֹב לְעוֹלָם אַל יְחַסְּרֵנוּ.

רַחֲמָן, הוּא יִמְלוֹךְ עָלֵינוּ לְעוֹלָם וָעֶד.

הָרַחֲמָן, הוּא יִתְבָּרַךְ בַּשָּׁמַיִם וּבָאָרֶץ.

הָרַחֲמָן, הוּא יִשְׁתַּבַּח לְדוֹר דּוֹרִים, וְיִתְפָּאַר בָּנוּ לָעַד וּלְנֵצַח נְצָחִים, וְיִתְהַדַּר בָּנוּ לָעַד וּלְעוֹלְמֵי עוֹלָמִים.

הָרַחֲמָן, הוּא יְפַרְנְסֵנוּ בְּכָבוֹד.

May the merciful Father end our oppression and lead the homeless of our people in dignity into our ancient homeland.

הָרַחֲמָן, הוּא יִשְׁבּוֹר עֻלֵנוּ מֵעַל צַוָּארֵנוּ, וְהוּא יוֹלִיכֵנוּ קוֹמְמִיּוּת לְאַרְצֵנוּ.

May the merciful Father grant abundant blessings upon this household and upon all who have eaten at this table [these tables].

הָרַחֲמָן, הוּא יִשְׁלַח בְּרָכָה מְרֻבָּה בַּבַּיִת הַזֶּה, וְעַל שֻׁלְחָן זֶה שֶׁאָכַלְנוּ עָלָיו.

May the merciful Father send us Elijah, the Prophet, be he remembered for his goodness; and may he announce to us good tidings of salvation and comfort.

הָרַחֲמָן, הוּא יִשְׁלַח לָנוּ אֶת אֵלִיָּהוּ הַנָּבִיא, זָכוּר לַטּוֹב, וִיבַשֶּׂר לָנוּ בְּשׂוֹרוֹת טוֹבוֹת, יְשׁוּעוֹת וְנֶחָמוֹת.

For Parents

May the merciful Father bless my revered father and teacher, and my esteemed mother and teacher, the heads of this household, them and all that is theirs.

הָרַחֲמָן, הוּא יְבָרֵךְ אֶת אָבִי מוֹרִי בַּעַל הַבַּיִת הַזֶּה וְאֶת אִמִּי מוֹרָתִי בַּעֲלַת הַבַּיִת הַזֶּה, אוֹתָם וְאֶת בֵּיתָם וְאֶת זַרְעָם וְאֶת כָּל אֲשֶׁר לָהֶם.

For the host

May the merciful Father bless our honored host, hostess and all their dear ones.

הָרַחֲמָן, הוּא יְבָרֵךְ אֶת בַּעַל הַבַּיִת וְאֶת אִשְׁתּוֹ בַּעֲלַת הַבַּיִת הַזֶּה, אוֹתָם וְאֶת בֵּיתָם וְאֶת זַרְעָם וְאֶת כָּל אֲשֶׁר לָהֶם.

For wife or husband

May the merciful Father bless me, my wife, [me, my husband], [my offspring], and all that is mine.

הָרַחֲמָן, הוּא יְבָרֵךְ אוֹתִי וְאֶת אִשְׁתִּי [אוֹתִי וְאֶת בַּעֲלִי] [וְאֶת זַרְעִי] וְאֶת כָּל אֲשֶׁר לִי.

For all those present

May the merciful Father bless all who are gathered at this table [these tables], them, their families, and all that is theirs.

הָרַחֲמָן, הוּא יְבָרֵךְ אֶת כָּל הַמְּסֻבִּין כַּאן, אוֹתָם וְאֶת זַרְעָם וְאֶת כָּל אֲשֶׁר לָהֶם.

May the merciful Father bless us and all who are dear to us, even as our fathers, Abraham, Isaac and Jacob were blessed, each with his own comprehensive blessing;* so, likewise, may He bless all of us together with a perfect blessing, and let us say, Amen.

הָרַחֲמָן, הוּא יְבָרֵךְ אוֹתָנוּ וְאֶת זַרְעֵנוּ וְאֶת כָּל אֲשֶׁר לָנוּ, כְּמוֹ שֶׁנִּתְבָּרְכוּ אֲבוֹתֵינוּ אַבְרָהָם יִצְחָק וְיַעֲקֹב בַּכֹּל, מִכֹּל, כֹּל, כֵּן יְבָרֵךְ אוֹתָנוּ כֻּלָּנוּ יַחַד בִּבְרָכָה שְׁלֵמָה, וְנֹאמַר אָמֵן.

May our merit and the merit of our fathers secure for all of us enduring peace. May we receive a blessing from the Lord, and mercy from the God of our salvation. May we find grace and favor in the sight of God and man.

בַּמָּרוֹם יְלַמְּדוּ עֲלֵיהֶם וְעָלֵינוּ זְכוּת, שֶׁתְּהֵא לְמִשְׁמֶרֶת שָׁלוֹם. וְנִשָּׂא בְרָכָה מֵאֵת יְיָ, וּצְדָקָה מֵאֱלֹהֵי יִשְׁעֵנוּ, וְנִמְצָא חֵן וְשֵׂכֶל טוֹב בְּעֵינֵי אֱלֹהִים וְאָדָם.

On Sabbath add:

May the merciful Father find us worthy of the uninterrupted Sabbath and serenity of the world to come.

הָרַחֲמָן, הוּא יַנְחִילֵנוּ יוֹם שֶׁכֻּלּוֹ שַׁבָּת וּמְנוּחָה לְחַיֵּי הָעוֹלָמִים.

May the merciful Father find us worthy of the time when complete felicity shall prevail.

הָרַחֲמָן, הוּא יַנְחִילֵנוּ יוֹם שֶׁכֻּלּוֹ טוֹב.

May the merciful Father find us worthy of the Messianic era and of the life to come.

הָרַחֲמָן, הוּא יְזַכֵּנוּ לִימוֹת הַמָּשִׁיחַ וּלְחַיֵּי הָעוֹלָם הַבָּא.

"He is a tower of deliverance to His (chosen) king, and shows kindness to His anointed one, to David and his descendants forever." (2 Sam. 22:51)

מִגְדּוֹל יְשׁוּעוֹת מַלְכּוֹ וְעֹשֶׂה חֶסֶד לִמְשִׁיחוֹ, לְדָוִד וּלְזַרְעוֹ עַד עוֹלָם.

May He, who makes peace in the heavenly spheres, grant peace to us, and to all Israel, and let us say, Amen.

עֹשֶׂה שָׁלוֹם בִּמְרוֹמָיו, הוּא יַעֲשֶׂה שָׁלוֹם עָלֵינוּ וְעַל כָּל יִשְׂרָאֵל, וְאִמְרוּ אָמֵן.

Migdol y'shuot malko v'oseh ḥesed li-m'sheeho, l'david u-l'zaro ad olam.
Oseh shalom bi-m'romav, hu ya-a-seh shalom alaynu v'al kol yisrael, v'imru amen.

---

* Gen. 24:1; 27:33; 33:11

Revere the Lord, you who are His holy ones; for those who revere Him suffer no want. Those who deny Him may lack food and suffer hunger, but they who seek the Lord shall not lack anything that is good. Give thanks unto the Lord for He is good; for His mercy endures forever. He opens His hand and satisfies every living thing with favor. Blessed is the man who trusts in the Lord; the Lord will be his protection. Once I was young, now I am old; yet I have not seen the righteous forsaken or his offspring begging for bread. The Lord will give strength to His people; the Lord will bless His people with peace. *

יְראוּ אֶת יְיָ קְדֹשָׁיו, כִּי אֵין מַחְסוֹר לִירֵאָיו. כְּפִירִים רָשׁוּ וְרָעֵבוּ, וְדֹרְשֵׁי יְיָ לֹא יַחְסְרוּ כָל טוֹב. הוֹדוּ לַיְיָ כִּי טוֹב, כִּי לְעוֹלָם חַסְדּוֹ. פּוֹתֵחַ אֶת יָדֶךָ, וּמַשְׂבִּיעַ לְכָל חַי רָצוֹן. בָּרוּךְ הַגֶּבֶר אֲשֶׁר יִבְטַח בַּיְיָ, וְהָיָה יְיָ מִבְטַחוֹ. נַעַר הָיִיתִי גַּם זָקַנְתִּי, וְלֹא רָאִיתִי צַדִּיק נֶעֱזָב, וְזַרְעוֹ מְבַקֶּשׁ לָחֶם. יְיָ עֹז לְעַמּוֹ יִתֵּן; יְיָ יְבָרֵךְ אֶת עַמּוֹ בַשָּׁלוֹם.

Drink the third cup of wine while reclining.

בָּרוּךְ אַתָּה יְיָ אֱלֹהֵינוּ מֶלֶךְ הָעוֹלָם בּוֹרֵא פְּרִי הַגָּפֶן:

Baruḥ atta Adonai, elohenu meleḥ ha-olam, boray p'ri ha-gafen.
Praised be Thou, O Lord our God, King of the Universe, Creator of the Fruit of the Vine.

The fourth cup of wine is filled.
The special cup for Elijah is also filled with wine.

The Haggadah opens with the words: "Let all who are hungry come and eat." Among the awaited guests is the prophet Elijah who, according to tradition, never died, but was carried up to heaven. The life of no other character in Jewish history is so surrounded with a halo of mystery and wonder as is that of Elijah. In Jewish legend, the ubiquitous Elijah is the champion of the oppressed; he brings hope, cheer and relief to the downtrodden; and he performs miracles of rescue and deliverance.

It is Elijah who can explain all difficult passages in the Bible and Talmud, and will settle all future controversies. The prophet Malachi says of him: "He will turn the hearts of parents to their children, and the hearts of children to their parents." Elijah is the harbinger of good tidings of joy and peace. His name is especially associated with the coming of the Messiah, whose advent he is expected to announce.

---

* Ps. 34:10; 118:1; 145:16; Jer. 17:7; Ps. 37:25; 29:11.

There is the legend that Elijah appears at every Seder and sips some wine from the cup reserved for him and, if the children are very observant, they may notice that after the door is closed, there is a little less wine in Elijah's cup.

Let us open the door and rise in the hope that Elijah will enter. With the salutation reserved for distinguished guests, let us say:

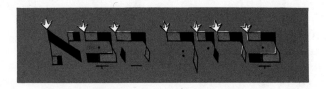

Blessed Be He Who Comes.

As we sing the song of Elijah, we pray that we may soon see fulfilled his hope of a world of freedom and peace for all mankind.

Elijah, the Prophet; Elijah, the Tishbite; Elijah, the Gileadite; may he soon come and bring the Messiah.	אֵלִיָּהוּ הַנָּבִיא, אֵלִיָּהוּ הַתִּשְׁבִּי, אֵלִיָּהוּ, אֵלִיָּהוּ, אֵלִיָּהוּ הַגִּלְעָדִי, בִּמְהֵרָה יָבֹא אֵלֵינוּ עִם מָשִׁיחַ בֶּן דָּוִד.

Eliyahu ha-navi, eliyahu ha-tishbee, eliyahu, eliyahu, eliyahu ha-giladi.
Bim'hay-ra b'ya-meynu, ya-vo ey-ley-nu, im mashiyaḥ ben david.

Alas, we now remember the thousands of Jews throughout our history for whom there was no deliverance. For centuries, our people were cruelly persecuted because they were determined to maintain their religious beliefs, traditions and ideals. Freedom of religion is comparatively new in our modern civilization. At one time Jews were maliciously accused of using the blood of Christians in the baking of unleavened bread.* Despite assurances by spiritual and temporal rulers, by popes and emperors, that such charges were false and absolutely without foundation, bigots utilized the accusation as a pretext for looting Jewish homes and shops and brutally massacring men, women and children. Some may recall the notorious trial of Mendel Beilis, against whom a "blood accusation" was made in Russia in 1911. The Jew did not retaliate against the inhumanities inflicted upon him. At the Seder, however, he vented his hurt and indignation through reciting the following Biblical verses:

"Pour out Thy wrath upon the heathen nations that do not acknowledge Thee and upon the kingdoms that do not call upon Thy name; for they have devoured Jacob and laid waste his dwelling place." (Ps. 79:6, 7)	שְׁפֹךְ חֲמָתְךָ אֶל הַגּוֹיִם אֲשֶׁר לֹא יְדָעוּךָ, וְעַל מַמְלָכוֹת אֲשֶׁר בְּשִׁמְךָ לֹא קָרָאוּ. כִּי אָכַל אֶת יַעֲקֹב, וְאֶת נָוֵהוּ הֵשַׁמּוּ.

---

* It is to be noted that the early Christians were accused by the pagans of using human blood in their ritual.

44

"Pour out upon them Thine indignation, and let Thy fury overtake them." (Ps. 69:25)

שְׁפָךְ עֲלֵיהֶם זַעְמֶךָ, וַחֲרוֹן אַפְּךָ יַשִּׂיגֵם.

"Pursue them in anger and destroy them from under the heavens of the Lord." (Lam. 3:66)

תִּרְדֹּף בְּאַף וְתַשְׁמִידֵם מִתַּחַת שְׁמֵי יְיָ.

The door is closed.

Leader

Let us now pause to recall the bitter catastrophe which so recently befell our people in Europe.

Responsive Reading

When in the past our brothers were massacred in ruthless pogroms, the poet Bialik, in his "City of Slaughter," cried out against the bloody savagery.

Today we mourn, not for one "city of slaughter" but for many such cities where six million of our people have been brutally destroyed.

The cruelties of Pharaoh, Haman, Nebuchadnezzar, and Titus, cannot be compared to the diabolical devices fashioned by modern tyrants in their design to exterminate a whole people.

No generation has known a catastrophe so vast and tragic!

The blood of the innocent, who perished in the gas-chambers of Auschwitz, Bergen-Belsen, Buchenwald, Dachau, Majdanek, Treblinka, and Theresienstadt, cries out to God and to man.

How can we ever forget the burning of synagogues and houses of study, the destruction of the holy books and scrolls of the Torah, the sadistic torment and murder of our scholars, sages, and teachers?

They tortured the flesh of our brothers, but they could not crush their spirit, their faith, nor their love of Torah.

The parchment of the Torah was burnt, but the letters were indestructible.

In the Warsaw Ghetto, Jews valiantly defied the overwhelming forces of the inhuman tyrant. These martyrs lifted up their voices in a hymn reaffirming their faith in the coming of the Messiah, when justice and peace shall finally be established for all men.

"I believe with a perfect faith in the coming of the Messiah; and though he tarry, nonetheless do I believe he will come!"

Anee ma-a-min b'emuna sh'lay-ma b'veeat ha-ma-shiah;
V'af al pee sheh-yitmah-maya, im kol zeh ahakeh lo b'hol yom sheh-yavo.

אֲנִי מַאֲמִין בֶּאֱמוּנָה שְׁלֵמָה בְּבִיאַת הַמָּשִׁיחַ;

וְאַף עַל פִּי שֶׁיִּתְמַהְמֵהַּ, עִם כָּל זֶה אֲחַכֶּה לוֹ בְּכָל יוֹם שֶׁיָּבֹא.

Let us pray: O Lord, remember Thy martyred children; remember all who have given their lives for KIDDUSH HASHEM, the sanctification of Thy name.

Grant their souls the peace reserved for all the righteous who are in Thy tender keeping.

And as we mourn our people's tragic fate, we also recall with admiration and gratitude the compassionate men and women of other faiths and nationalities who, at the peril of their lives, protected and saved thousands of Jews.

They are among those whom our Rabbis had in mind when they taught: "The righteous of all nations have a share in the world to come."

We are grateful to all the Allied Nations who liberated our people, and people of other faiths, from Nazi imprisonment, torture, and death.

With thankful hearts we shall ever remember the care and encouragement they gave to all those who were tragically displaced.

Let us all pray and work together for that day when there shall be no more violence or desolation anywhere on this earth.

"Nation shall not lift sword against nation; neither shall they learn war any more."

We who have witnessed the darkest chapter in modern Jewish history, have also witnessed our people's greatest triumph: the rebirth of the Jewish State.

We thank Thee, O Lord, that Thou hast permitted us to behold our people's return to Zion.

Thou hast opened the gates, and Thou didst "bring the remnant of Thy people from the east, and didst gather them from the west; Thou didst say to the north 'Give up!' and to the south 'Do not withhold them!'

"Thou didst bring Thy sons from afar, and Thy daughters from the ends of the earth!"

May we who live in this land of freedom, help our brothers to rebuild the State of Israel, that it may become secure and self-supporting, a stronghold of democracy, a bridge which unites the peoples of the East and of the West.

"For out of Zion shall go forth the Torah,
And the word of God from Jerusalem."

14. Hallel — RECITE THE HALLEL —

Hallel (Psalms of Praise) precedes and follows the festive meal to indicate that the meal is part of the religious service. Eating is not the mere consumption of food. In Judaism, the family meal is sanctified with prayer and D'VAR TORAH.

TRUST IN THE LORD!

Responsive Reading

PSALM 115:1–11   תהלים קטו, א–יא

Not for our sake, O Lord,
Not for our sake give glory,
But to reveal Thy love and Thy
truth.

לֹא לָנוּ, יְיָ, לֹא לָנוּ,
כִּי לְשִׁמְךָ תֵּן כָּבוֹד,
עַל חַסְדְּךָ, עַל אֲמִתֶּךָ.

   Why should the nations taunt
   us, saying:
   "Where now is their God?"

לָמָה יֹאמְרוּ הַגּוֹיִם,
אַיֵּה נָא אֱלֹהֵיהֶם?

Our God is in the heavens,
Doing whatsoever He desires.

וֵאלֹהֵינוּ בַשָּׁמָיִם;
כֹּל אֲשֶׁר חָפֵץ עָשָׂה.

   Their idols are mere silver and
   gold,
   The handiwork of men.

עֲצַבֵּיהֶם כֶּסֶף וְזָהָב,
מַעֲשֵׂה יְדֵי אָדָם.

They have mouths, but they
speak not;
Eyes have they, but they see not.

פֶּה לָהֶם וְלֹא יְדַבֵּרוּ,
עֵינַיִם לָהֶם וְלֹא יִרְאוּ.

   They have ears, but they hear
   not;
   Noses have they, but they
   breathe not.

אָזְנַיִם לָהֶם וְלֹא יִשְׁמָעוּ,
אַף לָהֶם וְלֹא יְרִיחוּן.

They have hands, but they touch
not;
Feet have they, but they walk not;
Neither can they utter a sound
with their throats.

יְדֵיהֶם וְלֹא יְמִישׁוּן,
רַגְלֵיהֶם וְלֹא יְהַלֵּכוּ;
לֹא יֶהְגּוּ בִּגְרוֹנָם.

   Whoever makes them shall become like them;
   Yea, every one that trusts in
   them.

כְּמוֹהֶם יִהְיוּ עֹשֵׂיהֶם,
כֹּל אֲשֶׁר בֹּטֵחַ בָּהֶם.

O Israel, trust in the Lord!
He is your help and your shield.

יִשְׂרָאֵל, בְּטַח בַּיְיָ;
עֶזְרָם וּמָגִנָּם הוּא.

47

House of Aaron, trust in the Lord!
He is your help and your shield.

You who revere the Lord, trust in the Lord!
He is your help and your shield.

בֵּית אַהֲרֹן, בִּטְחוּ בַיְיָ;
עֶזְרָם וּמָגִנָּם הוּא.

יִרְאֵי יְיָ, בִּטְחוּ בַיְיָ;
עֶזְרָם וּמָגִנָּם הוּא.

Only the Living Can Praise the Lord

PSALM 115:12–18

תהלים קטו, יב—יח

he Lord who has been mindful of us, will bless us;
He will bless the house of Israel;
He will bless the house of Aaron.

He will bless those who revere the Lord,
Both low and high alike.

יְיָ זְכָרָנוּ יְבָרֵךְ;
יְבָרֵךְ אֶת בֵּית יִשְׂרָאֵל,
יְבָרֵךְ אֶת בֵּית אַהֲרֹן.

יְבָרֵךְ יִרְאֵי יְיָ,
הַקְּטַנִּים עִם הַגְּדֹלִים.

May the Lord increase your numbers,
Yours and your children's.

יֹסֵף יְיָ עֲלֵיכֶם,
עֲלֵיכֶם וְעַל בְּנֵיכֶם.

Blessed may you be by the Lord,
Maker of heaven and earth.

בְּרוּכִים אַתֶּם לַיְיָ,
עֹשֵׂה שָׁמַיִם וָאָרֶץ.

The heavens are the heavens of the Lord,
But the earth has He given to the children of men.

The dead cannot praise the Lord,
Nor do any that go down into silence.

But we will praise the Lord,
From this time forth and forever.

הַשָּׁמַיִם שָׁמַיִם לַיְיָ,
וְהָאָרֶץ נָתַן לִבְנֵי אָדָם.

לֹא הַמֵּתִים יְהַלְלוּ יָהּ,
וְלֹא כָּל יֹרְדֵי דוּמָה.

וַאֲנַחְנוּ נְבָרֵךְ יָהּ
מֵעַתָּה וְעַד עוֹלָם;
הַלְלוּיָהּ !

Halleluyah!

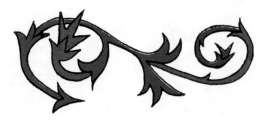

48

Responsive Reading

PSALM 116   תהלים קטז

I delight when the Lord hears
The voice of my supplications.

 אָהַבְתִּי כִּי יִשְׁמַע יְיָ

אֶת קוֹלִי תַּחֲנוּנָי.

Because He has inclined His ear
unto me,
Therefore will I call upon Him
all my days.

כִּי הִטָּה אָזְנוֹ לִי,

וּבְיָמַי אֶקְרָא.

The cords of death encircled me,
And the fear of the grave seized
me;
I was in anguish and despair.

אֲפָפוּנִי חֶבְלֵי מָוֶת,

וּמְצָרֵי שְׁאוֹל מְצָאוּנִי;

צָרָה וְיָגוֹן אֶמְצָא.

Then I called upon the Lord:
"O Lord, do Thou save me."

וּבְשֵׁם יְיָ אֶקְרָא,

אָנָּה יְיָ, מַלְּטָה נַפְשִׁי.

Gracious is the Lord, and righteous;
Yea, our God is merciful.

חַנּוּן יְיָ וְצַדִּיק,

וֵאלֹהֵינוּ מְרַחֵם.

The Lord guards the simple;
I was brought low and He saved
me.

שֹׁמֵר פְּתָאִים יְיָ;

דַּלּוֹתִי וְלִי יְהוֹשִׁיעַ.

Regain your tranquility, O my
soul,
For the Lord has dealt bountifully
with you,
For Thou, O Lord, hast deliv-
ered me from death,
Mine eyes from tears,
And my feet from stumbling.

שׁוּבִי נַפְשִׁי לִמְנוּחָיְכִי,

כִּי יְיָ גָּמַל עָלָיְכִי.

כִּי חִלַּצְתָּ נַפְשִׁי מִמָּוֶת,

אֶת עֵינִי מִן דִּמְעָה,

אֶת רַגְלִי מִדֶּחִי.

I shall walk before the Lord
In the land of the living.

אֶתְהַלֵּךְ לִפְנֵי יְיָ,

בְּאַרְצוֹת הַחַיִּים.

I had faith even when I cried
out:
"I am greatly afflicted."

הֶאֱמַנְתִּי כִּי אֲדַבֵּר,

אֲנִי עָנִיתִי מְאֹד.

And even when in panic I said:
"All men are deceitful."

אֲנִי אָמַרְתִּי בְחָפְזִי,

כָּל הָאָדָם כֹּזֵב.

What can I render unto the Lord,
For all His bounties to me?

מָה אָשִׁיב לַיְיָ
כָּל תַּגְמוּלוֹהִי עָלָי?

I will lift up the cup of salvation,
And call upon the name of the Lord.

כּוֹס יְשׁוּעוֹת אֶשָּׂא,
וּבְשֵׁם יְיָ אֶקְרָא.

My vows to the Lord will I fulfill,
In the presence of all His people.

נְדָרַי לַיְיָ אֲשַׁלֵּם,
נֶגְדָה נָּא לְכָל עַמּוֹ.

Grievous in the sight of the Lord
Is the death of His faithful ones.

יָקָר בְּעֵינֵי יְיָ
הַמָּוְתָה לַחֲסִידָיו.

Ah, Lord, I am indeed Thy servant;
I am Thy servant, the son of Thy handmaid;
Thou hast loosened my bonds.

אָנָּה יְיָ, כִּי אֲנִי עַבְדֶּךָ,
אֲנִי עַבְדְּךָ בֶּן אֲמָתֶךָ;
פִּתַּחְתָּ לְמוֹסֵרָי.

I will render Thee an offering of thanksgiving,
And will call upon the name of the Lord.

לְךָ אֶזְבַּח זֶבַח תּוֹדָה,
וּבְשֵׁם יְיָ אֶקְרָא.

My vows to the Lord will I fulfill,
In the presence of all His people,

נְדָרַי לַיְיָ אֲשַׁלֵּם,
נֶגְדָה נָּא לְכָל עַמּוֹ.

In the courts of the Lord's house,
In the midst of Jerusalem.

בְּחַצְרוֹת בֵּית יְיָ,
בְּתוֹכֵכִי יְרוּשָׁלָיִם;

Halleluyah!

הַלְלוּיָהּ !

GOD'S LOVINGKINDNESS IS EVERLASTING

Responsive Reading

Psalm 117

תהלים קיז

raise the Lord, all nations;
Extol Him, all peoples.

הַלְלוּ אֶת יְיָ, כָּל גּוֹיִם;
שַׁבְּחוּהוּ, כָּל הָאֻמִּים.

For great is His kindness toward us;
And His faithfulness is ever-lasting.
Halleluyah!

כִּי גָבַר עָלֵינוּ חַסְדּוֹ,
וֶאֱמֶת יְיָ לְעוֹלָם;
הַלְלוּיָהּ !

50

Give thanks to the Lord, for He is
good,
His lovingkindness is everlasting.

הוֹדוּ לַייָ כִּי טוֹב
כִּי לְעוֹלָם חַסְדּוֹ.

Let Israel now proclaim,
That His lovingkindness is everlasting.

יֹאמַר נָא יִשְׂרָאֵל
כִּי לְעוֹלָם חַסְדּוֹ.

Let the house of Aaron proclaim,
That His lovingkindness is everlasting.

יֹאמְרוּ נָא בֵית אַהֲרֹן
כִּי לְעוֹלָם חַסְדּוֹ.

Let those who revere the Lord
proclaim,
That His lovingkindness is everlasting.

יֹאמְרוּ נָא יִרְאֵי יְיָ
כִּי לְעוֹלָם חַסְדּוֹ.

Out of my distress I called upon
the Lord;
He answered me and set me free.

מִן הַמֵּצַר קָרֶאתִי יָּה,
עָנָנִי בַמֶּרְחָב יָהּ.

The Lord is with me, I will not
fear;
What can man do to me?

יְיָ לִי, לֹא אִירָא;
מַה יַּעֲשֶׂה לִי אָדָם?

The Lord is with me as my helper;
I shall see the downfall of mine
enemies,

יְיָ לִי בְּעֹזְרָי,
וַאֲנִי אֶרְאֶה בְשׂנְאָי.

It is better to rely upon the Lord
Than to depend upon man.

טוֹב לַחֲסוֹת בַּייָ
מִבְּטֹחַ בָּאָדָם.

It is better to rely upon the Lord
Than to depend upon princes.

טוֹב לַחֲסוֹת בַּייָ
מִבְּטֹחַ בִּנְדִיבִים.

Many nations encircled me;
In the name of the Lord I over-
came them.

כָּל גּוֹיִם סְבָבוּנִי;
בְּשֵׁם יְיָ, כִּי אֲמִילַם.

They encircled me all around;
In the name of the Lord I over-
came them.

סַבּוּנִי גַם סְבָבוּנִי;
בְּשֵׁם יְיָ, כִּי אֲמִילַם.

They swarmed about me like
bees;
They were quenched as a fire
among thorns;
In the name of the Lord I over-
came them.

סַבּוּנִי כִדְבֹרִים,
דֹּעֲכוּ כְּאֵשׁ קוֹצִים;
בְּשֵׁם יְיָ, כִּי אֲמִילַם.

51

They thrust at me to make me fall;
But the Lord came to my assistance.

The Lord is my strength and my song,
And He has become my deliverance.

Hark! This joyous song of victory
Is heard in the tents of the righteous:

"The might of the Lord is triumphant!
The power of the Lord is exalted!
The strength of the Lord is victorious!"

I shall not die, but live
To recount the works of the Lord.

The Lord has severely chastened me,
But He has not given me over to death.

Open to me the gates of righteousness,
That I may enter and praise the Lord.

This is the gate of the Lord;
The righteous alone shall enter.

דָּחֹה דְחִיתַנִי לִנְפֹּל,
וַיְיָ עֲזָרָנִי.

עָזִּי וְזִמְרָת יָהּ,
וַיְהִי לִי לִישׁוּעָה.

קוֹל רִנָּה וִישׁוּעָה
בְּאָהֳלֵי צַדִּיקִים;

יְמִין יְיָ עֹשָׂה חָיִל !
יְמִין יְיָ רוֹמֵמָה !
יְמִין יְיָ עֹשָׂה חָיִל !

לֹא אָמוּת כִּי אֶחְיֶה,
וַאֲסַפֵּר מַעֲשֵׂי יָהּ.

יַסֹּר יִסְּרַנִי יָּהּ,
וְלַמָּוֶת לֹא נְתָנָנִי.

פִּתְחוּ לִי שַׁעֲרֵי צֶדֶק;
אָבֹא בָם, אוֹדֶה יָהּ.

זֶה הַשַּׁעַר לַיְיָ,
צַדִּיקִים יָבֹאוּ בוֹ.

Each of the following verses is repeated.

I thank Thee, O Lord, that Thou hast answered me,
And art become my deliverance.

The stone which the builders rejected
Has become the chief cornerstone.

אוֹדְךָ כִּי עֲנִיתָנִי,
וַתְּהִי לִי לִישׁוּעָה.

אֶבֶן מָאֲסוּ הַבּוֹנִים,
הָיְתָה לְרֹאשׁ פִּנָּה.

This is the work of the Lord;
It is marvelous in our eyes.

מֵאֵת יְיָ הָיְתָה זֹּאת;
הִיא נִפְלָאת בְּעֵינֵינוּ.

This is the day which the Lord has made;
Let us rejoice and be glad thereon.

זֶה הַיּוֹם עָשָׂה יְיָ,
נָגִילָה וְנִשְׂמְחָה בוֹ.

We beseech Thee, O Lord, do Thou help us!
We beseech Thee, O Lord, do Thou prosper us!

אָנָּא יְיָ, הוֹשִׁיעָה נָּא.
אָנָּא יְיָ, הַצְלִיחָה נָא.

Blessed be he who comes in the name of the Lord;
We bless you from the house of the Lord.

בָּרוּךְ הַבָּא בְּשֵׁם יְיָ;
בֵּרַכְנוּכֶם מִבֵּית יְיָ.

The Lord is God; He has given us light;
Adorn the festival procession with myrtle boughs
To the very horns of the altar, (singing):

אֵל יְיָ וַיָּאֶר לָנוּ,
אִסְרוּ חַג בַּעֲבֹתִים,
עַד קַרְנוֹת הַמִּזְבֵּחַ.

"Thou art my God, and I will give thanks unto Thee;
Thou art my God; I will extol Thee.

אֵלִי אַתָּה וְאוֹדֶךָּ,
אֱלֹהַי אֲרוֹמְמֶךָּ.

Give thanks to the Lord, for He is good;
His lovingkindness is everlasting."

הוֹדוּ לַיְיָ כִּי טוֹב,
כִּי לְעוֹלָם חַסְדּוֹ.

Prayer Closing the Hallel

All Thy works shall praise Thee, O Lord our God, and Thy pious ones, the just who do Thy will, together with all Thy people, the house of Israel, shall praise Thee in joyous song. They shall thank, exalt, revere and sanctify Thee, and ascribe sovereignty to Thy name, O our King. For it is good to give thanks to Thee, and it is fitting to sing praises to Thy name, for Thou art God from everlasting to everlasting.

יְהַלְלוּךָ, יְיָ אֱלֹהֵינוּ, כָּל מַעֲשֶׂיךָ;
וַחֲסִידֶיךָ, צַדִּיקִים עוֹשֵׂי רְצוֹנֶךָ,
וְכָל עַמְּךָ בֵּית יִשְׂרָאֵל, בְּרִנָּה יוֹדוּ
וִיבָרְכוּ, וִישַׁבְּחוּ וִיפָאֲרוּ, וִירוֹמְמוּ
וְיַעֲרִיצוּ, וְיַקְדִּישׁוּ וְיַמְלִיכוּ אֶת שִׁמְךָ
מַלְכֵּנוּ. כִּי לְךָ טוֹב לְהוֹדוֹת, וּלְשִׁמְךָ
נָאֶה לְזַמֵּר, כִּי מֵעוֹלָם עַד עוֹלָם
אַתָּה אֵל. בָּרוּךְ אַתָּה, יְיָ, מֶלֶךְ
מְהֻלָּל בַּתִּשְׁבָּחוֹת.

53

וַלֵּל הַגָּדוֹל

THE GREAT HALLEL

Responsive Reading

PSALM 136

תהלים קלו

ive thanks to the Lord, for He is good; His lovingkindness is everlasting.

הוֹדוּ לַיְיָ, כִּי טוֹב,

כִּי לְעוֹלָם חַסְדּוֹ.

Give thanks to the supreme God;
Give thanks to the supreme Lord;
His lovingkindness is everlasting.

הוֹדוּ לֵאלֹהֵי הָאֱלֹהִים, כל"ח.

הוֹדוּ לַאֲדֹנֵי הָאֲדֹנִים, כל"ח.

Give thanks to Him alone who performs great wonders;
Whose wisdom made the heavens,
Who spread the earth over the waters,
And who made the heavenly lights,
The sun to rule by day,
The moon and the stars to rule by night;
His lovingkindness is everlasting.

לְעֹשֵׂה נִפְלָאוֹת גְּדֹלוֹת לְבַדּוֹ, כל"ח.

לְעֹשֵׂה הַשָּׁמַיִם בִּתְבוּנָה, כל"ח.

לְרוֹקַע הָאָרֶץ עַל הַמָּיִם, כל"ח.

לְעֹשֵׂה אוֹרִים גְּדֹלִים, כל"ח.

אֶת הַשֶּׁמֶשׁ לְמֶמְשֶׁלֶת בַּיּוֹם, כל"ח.

אֶת הַיָּרֵחַ וְכוֹכָבִים לְמֶמְשְׁלוֹת בַּלָּיְלָה, כל"ח.

He smote Egypt through their first-born,
And brought out Israel from among them,
With a strong hand and an out-stretched arm;
His lovingkindness is everlasting.

לְמַכֵּה מִצְרַיִם בִּבְכוֹרֵיהֶם, כל"ח.

וַיּוֹצֵא יִשְׂרָאֵל מִתּוֹכָם, כל"ח.

בְּיָד חֲזָקָה וּבִזְרוֹעַ נְטוּיָה, כל"ח.

He divided the Red Sea,
And led Israel safely through it;
But He overthrew Pharaoh and his army in the Red Sea.
He led His people through the wilderness;
His lovingkindness is everlasting.

לְגֹזֵר יַם סוּף לִגְזָרִים, כל"ח.

וְהֶעֱבִיר יִשְׂרָאֵל בְּתוֹכוֹ, כל"ח.

וְנִעֵר פַּרְעֹה וְחֵילוֹ בְיַם סוּף, כל"ח.

לְמוֹלִיךְ עַמּוֹ בַּמִּדְבָּר, כל"ח.

He smote great kings who oppressed us,
And struck down these mighty kings:
Sihon, king of the Amorites,
And Og, king of Bashan,

לְמַכֵּה מְלָכִים גְּדֹלִים, כל"ח.

וַיַּהֲרֹג מְלָכִים אַדִּירִים, כל"ח.

לְסִיחוֹן מֶלֶךְ הָאֱמֹרִי, כל"ח.

וּלְעוֹג מֶלֶךְ הַבָּשָׁן, כל"ח.

54

And He gave their land as a heritage,	כְּל"חַ.	וְנָתַן אַרְצָם לְנַחֲלָה,
A heritage to Israel, His servant; His lovingkindness is everlasting.	כְּל"חַ.	נַחֲלָה לְיִשְׂרָאֵל עַבְדּוֹ,
He remembered us when we were downcast,	כְּל"חַ.	שֶׁבְּשִׁפְלֵנוּ זָכַר לָנוּ,
And redeemed us from our foes; His lovingkindness is everlasting.	כְּל"חַ.	וַיִּפְרְקֵנוּ מִצָּרֵינוּ,
He gives food to all creatures; His lovingkindness is everlasting.	כְּל"חַ.	נֹתֵן לֶחֶם לְכָל בָּשָׂר,

Give thanks to the God of heaven;

His lovingkindness is everlasting.

הוֹדוּ לְאֵל הַשָּׁמַיִם,

כִּי לְעוֹלָם חַסְדּוֹ.

All things that live shall praise
    Thy name,
The spirit of all flesh proclaim
Thy sovereignty, O Lord our God.

    From everlasting Thou art God,
    To everlasting Thou shalt be;
    We have no other God but Thee.

Thy goodness and Thy holiness
Support us in all times of stress,
Redeemer, Lord and King.

    Thou art the God of first and
      last,
    In every age Thy children raise
    Their voices in eternal praise.

With tender love Thy world dost
    guide,
And for our needs dost Thou pro-
    vide;
Thou keepest watch eternally.

    Thou takest slumber from our
      eyes,
    And to the speechless givest
      voice;
    Through Thy great mercy all
      rejoice.

Thou raisest those whose heads
    are bent,
Sustaining all the weak and
    spent;
To Thee alone we render thanks.

    If like the sea our mouths could
      sing,
    Our tongues like murmuring
      waves implore,
    Our lips like spacious skies
      adore;

And were our eyes like moon or
    sun,
Our hands like eagles' wings upon
The heavens, to spread and reach
    to Thee;

נִשְׁמַת כָּל חַי תְּבָרֵךְ אֶת שִׁמְךָ, יְיָ אֱלֹהֵינוּ, וְרוּחַ כָּל בָּשָׂר תְּפָאֵר וּתְרוֹמֵם זִכְרְךָ, מַלְכֵּנוּ, תָּמִיד. מִן הָעוֹלָם וְעַד הָעוֹלָם אַתָּה אֵל, וּמִבַּלְעָדֶיךָ אֵין לָנוּ מֶלֶךְ גּוֹאֵל וּמוֹשִׁיעַ, פּוֹדֶה וּמַצִּיל וּמְפַרְנֵס, וּמְרַחֵם בְּכָל עֵת צָרָה וְצוּקָה; אֵין לָנוּ מֶלֶךְ אֶלָּא אָתָּה. אֱלֹהֵי הָרִאשׁוֹנִים וְהָאַחֲרוֹנִים, אֱלוֹהַּ כָּל בְּרִיוֹת, אֲדוֹן כָּל תּוֹלָדוֹת, הַמְהֻלָּל בְּרֹב הַתִּשְׁבָּחוֹת, הַמְנַהֵג עוֹלָמוֹ בְּחֶסֶד וּבְרִיּוֹתָיו בְּרַחֲמִים. וַיְיָ לֹא יָנוּם וְלֹא יִישָׁן, הַמְעוֹרֵר יְשֵׁנִים, וְהַמֵּקִיץ נִרְדָּמִים, וְהַמֵּשִׂיחַ אִלְּמִים, וְהַמַּתִּיר אֲסוּרִים, וְהַסּוֹמֵךְ נוֹפְלִים, וְהַזּוֹקֵף כְּפוּפִים. לְךָ לְבַדְּךָ אֲנַחְנוּ מוֹדִים.

אִלּוּ פִינוּ מָלֵא שִׁירָה כַיָּם, וּלְשׁוֹנֵנוּ רִנָּה כַּהֲמוֹן גַּלָּיו, וְשִׂפְתוֹתֵינוּ שֶׁבַח כְּמֶרְחֲבֵי רָקִיעַ, וְעֵינֵינוּ מְאִירוֹת כַּשֶּׁמֶשׁ וְכַיָּרֵחַ, וְיָדֵינוּ פְרוּשׂוֹת כְּנִשְׁרֵי

And if our feet were swift as hinds,
Yet would we still unable be
To thank Thee, God, sufficiently;
To thank Thee for one-thousandth share
Of all Thy kind and loving care
Which Thou in every age hast shown.

From Egypt didst Thou lead us forth,
From bondage didst Thou set us free,
Redeeming us from slavery.

In famine, food didst Thou provide,
In plenty, Thou wast at our side,
To keep and guide us, Lord our God.

From pestilence and sword didst save,
And when we were by ills assailed,
Thy love and mercy never failed.

O Lord, Thy wondrous deeds we praise,
Forsake us not throughout our days;
Be Thou our help forevermore.

Therefore, O Lord, our limbs, our breath,
Our soul, our tongue, shall all proclaim
Thy praise, and glorify Thy name;

And every mouth and every tongue
Declare allegiance without end;
And every knee to Thee shall bend.

The mighty ones shall humble be,
Yea, every heart revere but Thee,
And sing the glory of Thy name.

שָׁמַיִם, וְרַגְלֵינוּ קַלּוֹת כָּאַיָּלוֹת, אֵין

אֲנַחְנוּ מַסְפִּיקִים לְהוֹדוֹת לְךָ, יְיָ

אֱלֹהֵינוּ וֵאלֹהֵי אֲבוֹתֵינוּ, וּלְבָרֵךְ אֶת

שְׁמֶךָ עַל אַחַת מֵאֶלֶף (אֶלֶף) אַלְפֵי

אֲלָפִים וְרִבֵּי רְבָבוֹת פְּעָמִים הַטּוֹבוֹת

שֶׁעָשִׂיתָ עִם אֲבוֹתֵינוּ וְעִמָּנוּ. מִמִּצְרַיִם

גְּאַלְתָּנוּ, יְיָ אֱלֹהֵינוּ, וּמִבֵּית עֲבָדִים

פְּדִיתָנוּ; בְּרָעָב זַנְתָּנוּ וּבְשָׂבָע

כִּלְכַּלְתָּנוּ; מֵחֶרֶב הִצַּלְתָּנוּ וּמִדֶּבֶר

מִלַּטְתָּנוּ, וּמֵחֳלָיִם רָעִים וְנֶאֱמָנִים

דִּלִּיתָנוּ. עַד הֵנָּה עֲזָרוּנוּ רַחֲמֶיךָ

וְלֹא עֲזָבוּנוּ חֲסָדֶיךָ; וְאַל תִּטְּשֵׁנוּ,

יְיָ אֱלֹהֵינוּ, לָנֶצַח. עַל כֵּן, אֵבָרִים

שֶׁפִּלַּגְתָּ בָּנוּ, וְרוּחַ וּנְשָׁמָה שֶׁנָּפַחְתָּ

בְּאַפֵּינוּ, וְלָשׁוֹן אֲשֶׁר שַׂמְתָּ בְּפִינוּ, הֵן

הֵם יוֹדוּ וִיבָרְכוּ, וִישַׁבְּחוּ וִיפָאֲרוּ,

וִירוֹמְמוּ וְיַעֲרִיצוּ, וְיַקְדִּישׁוּ וְיַמְלִיכוּ

אֶת שִׁמְךָ, מַלְכֵּנוּ. כִּי כָל פֶּה לְךָ

יוֹדֶה, וְכָל לָשׁוֹן לְךָ תִשָּׁבַע, וְכָל

בֶּרֶךְ לְךָ תִכְרַע, וְכָל קוֹמָה לְפָנֶיךָ

תִשְׁתַּחֲוֶה. וְכָל לְבָבוֹת יִירָאוּךָ, וְכָל

קֶרֶב וּכְלָיוֹת יְזַמְּרוּ לִשְׁמֶךָ, כַּדָּבָר

In the words of the Psalmist: "My whole being shall proclaim: 'O Lord, who is like Thee? Thou deliverest the weak from him who is stronger, the poor and the needy from his despoiler.'" (35:10)

Who is like Thee, who is equal to Thee, who can be compared to Thee, O great, mighty, revered and supreme God, Creator of heaven and earth? We will praise, laud, and glorify Thee; we will extol Thy holy name in the words of the Psalm of David: "Praise the Lord, O my soul, and all that is within me, praise His holy name." (103:1)

Thou art God by the power of Thy might; Thou art great by the glory of Thy name; Thou art mighty unto everlasting, and revered for Thine awe-inspiring works; Thou art King, enthroned on high.

Thou who abidest in eternity, Thy name is "Exalted and Holy." As the Psalmist declared: "Rejoice in the Lord, O ye righteous; it is befitting for the upright to praise Him." (33:1)

By the mouth of the upright,
Thou shalt be glorified;
By the words of the righteous,
Thou shalt be praised;
By the tongue of the faithful,
Thou shalt be extolled;
And in the midst of the holy,
Thou shalt be sanctified.

שֶׁכָּתוּב: כָּל עַצְמוֹתַי תֹּאמַרְנָה, יְיָ מִי כָמְוֹךָ? מַצִּיל עָנִי מֵחָזָק מִמֶּנּוּ, וְעָנִי וְאֶבְיוֹן מִגֹּזְלוֹ. מִי יִדְמֶה לָּךְ, וּמִי יִשְׁוֶה לָּךְ, וּמִי יַעֲרָךְ לָךְ, הָאֵל הַגָּדוֹל, הַגִּבּוֹר וְהַנּוֹרָא, אֵל עֶלְיוֹן, קֹנֵה שָׁמַיִם וָאָרֶץ? נְהַלֶּלְךָ וּנְשַׁבֵּחֲךָ וּנְפָאֶרְךָ, וּנְבָרֵךְ אֶת שֵׁם קָדְשֶׁךָ, כָּאָמוּר: לְדָוִד, בָּרְכִי נַפְשִׁי אֶת יְיָ, וְכָל קְרָבַי אֶת שֵׁם קָדְשׁוֹ.

הָאֵל בְּתַעֲצֻמוֹת עֻזֶּךָ, הַגָּדוֹל בִּכְבוֹד שְׁמֶךָ, הַגִּבּוֹר לָנֶצַח וְהַנּוֹרָא בְּנוֹרְאוֹתֶיךָ, הַמֶּלֶךְ הַיּוֹשֵׁב עַל כִּסֵּא רָם וְנִשָּׂא.

שׁוֹכֵן עַד, מָרוֹם וְקָדוֹשׁ שְׁמוֹ. וְכָתוּב: רַנְּנוּ צַדִּיקִים בַּיְיָ, לַיְשָׁרִים נָאוָה תְהִלָּה.

בְּפִי יְשָׁרִים תִּתְהַלָּל,

וּבְדִבְרֵי צַדִּיקִים תִּתְבָּרַךְ,

וּבִלְשׁוֹן חֲסִידִים תִּתְרוֹמָם,

וּבְקֶרֶב קְדוֹשִׁים תִּתְקַדָּשׁ.

58

In the assembled multitudes of Thy people, the house of Israel, Thy name, O our King, shall be glorified with song in every generation. For it is the duty of all creatures, O Lord our God and God of our fathers, to thank, laud, adore and praise Thee, even beyond all the words of song and praise uttered by David, son of Jesse, Thine anointed servant.

raised be Thy name forever, O our King, our divine Sovereign, great and holy in heaven and on earth. For to Thee are due, O Lord our God and God of our fathers, song and praise, hymn and psalm, acclaiming Thy power and dominion, victory and glory, holiness and sovereignty. To Thee we offer praise and thanksgiving from this time forth and forevermore. Praised be Thou, exalted God, our King, to whom our thanks are due; Lord of wondrous deeds, who delightest in hymns of praise, Thou art God and King, the life of the universe.

וּבְמַקְהֲלוֹת רִבְבוֹת עַמְּךָ בֵּית יִשְׂרָאֵל בְּרִנָּה יִתְפָּאַר שִׁמְךָ, מַלְכֵּנוּ, בְּכָל דּוֹר וָדוֹר; שֶׁכֵּן חוֹבַת כָּל הַיְצוּרִים לְפָנֶיךָ, יְיָ אֱלֹהֵינוּ וֵאלֹהֵי אֲבוֹתֵינוּ, לְהוֹדוֹת, לְהַלֵּל, לְשַׁבֵּחַ, לְפָאֵר, לְרוֹמֵם, לְהַדֵּר, לְבָרֵךְ, לְעַלֵּה וּלְקַלֵּס עַל כָּל דִּבְרֵי שִׁירוֹת וְתִשְׁבְּחוֹת דָּוִד בֶּן יִשַׁי עַבְדְּךָ מְשִׁיחֶךָ.

יִשְׁתַּבַּח שִׁמְךָ לָעַד, מַלְכֵּנוּ, הָאֵל הַמֶּלֶךְ הַגָּדוֹל וְהַקָּדוֹשׁ, בַּשָּׁמַיִם וּבָאָרֶץ. כִּי לְךָ נָאֶה, יְיָ אֱלֹהֵינוּ וֵאלֹהֵי אֲבוֹתֵינוּ, שִׁיר וּשְׁבָחָה, הַלֵּל וְזִמְרָה, עֹז וּמֶמְשָׁלָה, נֶצַח, גְּדֻלָּה וּגְבוּרָה, תְּהִלָּה וְתִפְאֶרֶת, קְדֻשָׁה וּמַלְכוּת, בְּרָכוֹת וְהוֹדָאוֹת, מֵעַתָּה וְעַד עוֹלָם. בָּרוּךְ אַתָּה, יְיָ, אֵל מֶלֶךְ גָּדוֹל בַּתִּשְׁבָּחוֹת, אֵל הַהוֹדָאוֹת, אֲדוֹן הַנִּפְלָאוֹת, הַבּוֹחֵר בְּשִׁירֵי זִמְרָה, מֶלֶךְ, אֵל, חַי הָעוֹלָמִים.

For the First Seder Night

The following PIYYUT (poem) in alphabetical acrostic was probably composed in the seventh century by Rabbi Yannai. The poet fancifully enumerates miracles in Biblical history which, according to tradition, occurred at midnight. He concludes with the hope of ultimate redemption, to take place on Passover night. The refrain, "It came to pass at midnight," is from Exodus 12:29.

And it Came to Pass at Midnight.

וּבְכֵן, וַיְהִי בַּחֲצִי הַלַּיְלָה.

In the days of old didst Thou perform many miracles at night.
In the early watch of evening, on this night, To gain the victory, Abraham divided his army at night. (Gen. 14:15)
     And it came to pass at midnight.

אָז רוֹב נִסִּים הִפְלֵאתָ בַּלַּיְלָה,
בְּ רֹאשׁ אַשְׁמוּרוֹת זֶה הַלַּיְלָה,
גֵּ ר צֶדֶק נִצַּחְתּוֹ כְּנֶחֱלַק לוֹ לַיְלָה.
וַיְהִי בַּחֲצִי הַלַּיְלָה.

Thou didst judge Abimelech, king of Gerar, in a dream during the night; (Gen. 20:3)
Thou didst strike Laban, the Syrian, with terror in the night; (Gen. 31:24)
Israel wrestled with an angel, and prevailed at night. (Gen. 32:25)
     And it came to pass at midnight.

דַּ נְתָּ מֶלֶךְ גְּרָר בַּחֲלוֹם הַלַּיְלָה,
הִ פְחַדְתָּ אֲרַמִּי בְּאֶמֶשׁ לַיְלָה,
וַ יֵּשַׂר יִשְׂרָאֵל לְמַלְאָךְ וַיּוּכַל לוֹ לַיְלָה.
וַיְהִי בַּחֲצִי הַלַּיְלָה.

Egypt's first-born didst Thou smite at night; (Ex. 12:29)
The Egyptians found themselves powerless when they arose at night.
Sisera's army didst Thou scatter, aided by the stars of night. (Judg. 5:20)
     It came to pass at midnight.

זֶ רַע בְּכוֹרֵי פַתְרוֹס מָחַצְתָּ בַּחֲצִי הַלַּיְלָה,
חֵ ילָם לֹא מָצְאוּ בְּקוּמָם בַּלַּיְלָה,
טִ יסַת נְגִיד חֲרֹשֶׁת סִלִּיתָ בְּכוֹכְבֵי לַיְלָה.
וַיְהִי בַּחֲצִי הַלַּיְלָה.

Sennacherib's army was decimated at night; (2 Ki. 19:35)
Babylonia's god, Bel, and his pillar crashed in the night; (Is. 46:1, 2)
Mysteries were revealed to Daniel in a vision at night. (Dan. 2:19)
     It came to pass at midnight.

יָ עַץ מְחָרֵף לְנוֹפֵף אִוּוּי הוֹבַשְׁתָּ פְגָרָיו בַּלַּיְלָה,
כָּ רַע בֵּל וּמַצָּבוֹ בְּאִישׁוֹן לַיְלָה,
לְ אִישׁ חֲמוּדוֹת נִגְלָה רָז חֲזוֹת לַיְלָה.
וַיְהִי בַּחֲצִי הַלַּיְלָה.

Drunken Balshazzar was slain at night; (Dan. 5:30)
Daniel, saved from the lions' den, interpreted the dreams of night. (Dan. 6:24)
Hateful Haman wrote his edicts at night. (Esth. 3:12)
     It came to pass at midnight.

מִ שְׁתַּכֵּר בִּכְלֵי קֹדֶשׁ נֶהֱרַג בּוֹ בַּלַּיְלָה,
נוֹ שַׁע מִבּוֹר אֲרָיוֹת פּוֹתֵר בִּעֲתוּתֵי לַיְלָה,
שִׂ נְאָה נָטַר אֲגָגִי וְכָתַב סְפָרִים בַּלַּיְלָה.
וַיְהִי בַּחֲצִי הַלַּיְלָה.

60

Thou didst triumph over Haman when sleep failed Ahasuerus at night. (Esth. 6:1)
Thou didst tread down the enemy for him who asked: "Watchman, what of the night?" (Is. 63:3; 21:11)
Thou wilt answer like the watchman: "The morning comes as well as the night." (Is. 21:12)
    It came to pass at midnight.

Hasten that day which is neither day nor night; (Zech. 14:7)
Most High, proclaim that Thine is the day, and Thine is also the night.
Place watchmen to guard the city, day and night. (Is. 62:6)
Make bright as day the darkness of the night.
    May it come to pass at midnight.

עוֹרַרְתָּ נִצְחֲךָ עָלָיו בְּנֶדֶד שְׁנַת לַיְלָה,

פּוּרָה תִדְרוֹךְ לְשׁוֹמֵר מַה מִלַּיְלָה,

צָרַח כַּשּׁוֹמֵר וְשָׂח אָתָא בְקֶר וְגַם לַיְלָה.

וַיְהִי בַּחֲצִי הַלַּיְלָה.

קָרֵב יוֹם אֲשֶׁר הוּא לֹא יוֹם וְלֹא לַיְלָה,

רָם הוֹדַע כִּי לְךָ הַיּוֹם אַף לְךָ הַלַּיְלָה,

שׁוֹמְרִים הַפְקֵד לְעִירְךָ כָּל הַיּוֹם וְכָל הַלַּיְלָה,

תָּאִיר כְּאוֹר יוֹם חֶשְׁכַת לַיְלָה.

וַיְהִי בַּחֲצִי הַלַּיְלָה.

For the Second Seder Night

    The following PIYYUT, in alphabetical acrostic, written in the eighth century by Rabbi Eleazar Ha-Kalir, a pupil of Rabbi Yannai, recounts the various deliverances that, according to Midrashic interpretation, took place at the Passover season. The refrain, "This is the Offering of Passover," is from Exodus 12:27.

You shall say:

This is the offering of Passover.

וּבְכֵן,

וַאֲמַרְתֶּם זֶבַח פֶּסַח.

The power of Thy might Thou didst reveal on Passover;
Above all other festivals didst Thou place the Passover;
To Abraham Thou didst reveal the midnight marvels of the Passover. (Baba Bathra 15a)
    This is the offering of Passover.

אֹמֶץ גְּבוּרוֹתֶיךָ הִפְלֵאתָ בַּפֶּסַח,

בְּרֹאשׁ כָּל מוֹעֲדוֹת נִשֵּׂאתָ פֶּסַח,

גִּלִּיתָ לְאֶזְרָחִי חֲצוֹת לֵיל פֶּסַח.

וַאֲמַרְתֶּם זֶבַח פֶּסַח.

To his door Thou didst come at midday's heat on Passover;
He served the angels with unleavened bread on Passover;
And to the herd he ran, to fetch a calf for Passover. (Gen. 18:1, 6, 7)
    This is the offering of Passover.

דְּלָתָיו דָּפַקְתָּ כְּחֹם הַיּוֹם בַּפֶּסַח,

הִסְעִיד נוֹצְצִים עֻגּוֹת מַצּוֹת בַּפֶּסַח,

וְאֶל הַבָּקָר רָץ זֵכֶר לְשׁוֹר עֵרֶךְ פֶּסַח.

וַאֲמַרְתֶּם זֶבַח פֶּסַח.

61

The wicked men of Sodom were consumed
by fire on Passover;
But Lot was saved, and baked unleavened
bread on Passover. (Gen. 19:3)
Thou didst sweep away the power of Egypt
on Passover.
     This is the offering of Passover.

O Lord, Thou didst smite the first-born of
Egypt on the night of Passover;
O Mighty One, Thy first-born didst Thou
spare on Passover;
Death passed over Israel's marked doors
on Passover. (Ex. 12:23)
     This is the offering of Passover.

The walled city of Jericho crashed on Passover. (Josh. 6:5)
Through a dream of barley cake, Midian
was destroyed on Passover. (Judg. 7:13)
The mighty Assyrian hordes were consumed
in blazing flame on Passover. (Midrash Yal.
Shim.)
     This is the offering of Passover.

Sennacherib, at Zion's gate, met disaster
on Passover. (Is. 10:32)
Upon the wall, a hand wrote Babylon's fate
on Passover. (Dan. 5:24)
"The watch is set; the table is spread" —
(Is. 21:5)
Feasting Babylon met her doom on Passover.
     This is the offering of Passover.

A three-day fast Queen Esther imposed on
Passover. (Esth. 4:16)
The wicked Haman was hung on gallows
fifty cubits high on Passover. (Esth. 7:9)
A double punishment shalt Thou bring upon
our foes on Passover. (Is. 47:9)
Thy hand is strong, Thy right hand uplifted,
Thy might shall again prevail on Passover.
(Ps. 89:14)
     This is the offering of Passover.

ז עֲמוּ סְדוֹמִים וְלֹהֲטוּ בָאֵשׁ בַּפֶּסַח,

ח לַץ לוֹט מֵהֶם וּמַצּוֹת אָפָה בְּקֵץ פֶּסַח,

ט אִטֵּאתָ אַדְמַת מֹף וְנֹף בְּעָבְרְךָ בַּפֶּסַח.

וַאֲמַרְתֶּם זֶבַח פֶּסַח.

י הּ רֹאשׁ כָּל אוֹן מָחַצְתָּ בְּלֵיל שִׁמּוּר פֶּסַח,

כַּ בִּיר עַל בֵּן בְּכוֹר פָּסַחְתָּ בְּדַם פֶּסַח,

לְ בִלְתִּי תֵּת מַשְׁחִית לָבֹא בִּפְתָחַי בַּפֶּסַח.

וַאֲמַרְתֶּם זֶבַח פֶּסַח.

מְ סֻגֶּרֶת סֻגָּרָה בְּעִתּוֹתֵי פֶּסַח,

נְ שְׁמְדָה מִדְיָן בִּצְלִיל שְׂעוֹרֵי עֹמֶר פֶּסַח,

שׁ רְפוּ מִשְׁמַנֵּי פּוּל וְלוּד בִּיקַד יְקוֹד פֶּסַח.

וַאֲמַרְתֶּם זֶבַח פֶּסַח.

ע וֹד הַיּוֹם בְּנֹב לַעֲמוֹד עַד גָּעָה עוֹנַת פֶּסַח,

פַּ ס יָד כָּתְבָה לְקַעֲקֵעַ צוּל בַּפֶּסַח,

צָ פֹה הַצָּפִית עָרוֹךְ הַשֻּׁלְחָן בַּפֶּסַח.

וַאֲמַרְתֶּם זֶבַח פֶּסַח.

קָ הָל כִּנְּסָה הֲדַסָּה צוֹם לְשַׁלֵּשׁ בַּפֶּסַח,

ר אֹשׁ מִבֵּית רָשָׁע מָחַצְתָּ בְּעֵץ חֲמִשִּׁים
בַּפֶּסַח,

שׁ תֵּי אֵלֶּה רֶגַע תָּבִיא לְעוּצִית בַּפֶּסַח,

תָּ עֹז יָדְךָ תָּרוּם יְמִינֶךָ כְּלֵיל הִתְקַדֶּשׁ חַג
פֶּסַח.

וַאֲמַרְתֶּם זֶבַח פֶּסַח.

Sefirah — COUNTING THE OMER — סְפִירָה

The ancient custom of counting the days for seven weeks beginning with the second night of Passover, recalls the agricultural life of our people, when each year they brought to the Sanctuary a measure (OMER) of their first barley harvest. (Lev. 23:10, 15, 16; Deut. 16:9)

This observance serves to strengthen our resolve to continue reclaiming the soil of the Holy Land and to work for the rebuilding of Zion as a homeland for the homeless, and as a center of spiritual life for our people.

According to Midrashic lore, the Israelites were told that fifty days after their liberation, they would receive the Torah on Mount Sinai. Just as one impatiently counts the days before a birthday, a wedding, or any other happy event, the Israelites, eager for that memorable occasion, began to count the days, saying each day: "Now there is one day less to wait before we receive the Torah."

Thus the Bible prescribed the counting of the days for seven weeks, from Passover to Shavuot, the festival which commemorates the giving of the Torah. The custom of counting the days of the OMER is the bridge connecting the two festivals: Pesah and Shavuot. Our Sages stressed not only freedom *from* bondage, but freedom *for* a purpose. Freedom is not enough. It must lead to the Torah. Without Law, freedom will not endure. The exodus from Egypt and the giving of the Ten Commandments on Mount Sinai, emphasize the nexus between freedom and the moral law.

Praised be Thou, O Lord our God, King of the universe, who hast sanctified us with Thy commandments and enjoined upon us the mitzvah of counting the OMER.

בָּרוּךְ אַתָּה, יְיָ אֱלֹהֵינוּ, מֶלֶךְ הָעוֹלָם, אֲשֶׁר קִדְּשָׁנוּ בְּמִצְוֹתָיו וְצִוָּנוּ עַל סְפִירַת הָעֹמֶר:

This is the first day of the OMER.

הַיּוֹם יוֹם אֶחָד לָעֹמֶר:

May it be Thy will, O Lord our God and God of our fathers, that the Temple be rebuilt speedily and in our lifetime, and may our portion be in Thy Torah.

יְהִי רָצוֹן מִלְּפָנֶיךָ, יְיָ אֱלֹהֵינוּ וֵאלֹהֵי אֲבוֹתֵינוּ, שֶׁיִּבָּנֶה בֵּית הַמִּקְדָּשׁ בִּמְהֵרָה בְיָמֵינוּ. וְתֵן חֶלְקֵנוּ בְּתוֹרָתֶךָ:

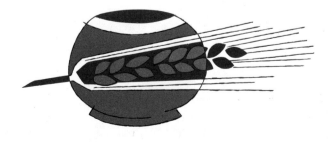

63

The Fourth Cup of Wine

There are several explanations why we drink four cups of wine at the Seder. The four cups correspond to the four letters of God's name: YOD HEH VAV HEH (Jehovah) — to indicate that God, the Liberator, is the Author of our freedom.

They mark the four divisions of the Seder service: the Kiddush; the reading of the Haggadah; the BIRKAT HAMAZON (blessing after the meal); and the concluding psalms and prayers.

The Bible uses four different expressions for the redemption of the Israelites from Egyptian bondage:

1. וְהוֹצֵאתִי — v'HO-TZE-TI, *"and I will bring you out* from under the burdens of the Egyptians."

2. וְהִצַּלְתִּי — v'HI-TZAL-TI, *"and I will deliver you* from their bondage."

3. וְגָאַלְתִּי — v'GA-AL-TI, *"and I will redeem you* with an outstretched arm, and with great judgments."

4. וְלָקַחְתִּי — v'LA-KAH-TI, *"and I will take you* to Me for a people."* (Ex. 6:6, 7)

These four expressions have been interpreted to refer to political, economic, intellectual and spiritual freedom. To be truly free, and to reach our highest potential, we must be free from want; free from all forms of oppression and tyranny; free in mind and spirit; and free to develop all the gifts with which God has endowed us.

After reciting the following blessing, drink the fourth cup of wine while reclining.

בָּרוּךְ אַתָּה יְיָ אֱלֹהֵינוּ מֶלֶךְ הָעוֹלָם בּוֹרֵא פְּרִי הַגָּפֶן׃

Baruh atta Adonai, elohenu meleh ha-olam, boray p'ri ha-gafen.

Praised be Thou, O Lord our God, King of the Universe, Creator of the Fruit of the Vine.

On Sabbath add words in brackets.

Praised be Thou, O Lord our God, King of the universe, for the vine and for the fruit of the vine, for the produce of the field and for the pleasant and spacious land which Thou, in Thy favor, didst grant to our fathers as an inheritance that they might eat of its fruit and enjoy its bounty. Remember in mercy, O Lord our God, Israel Thy people, Jerusalem Thy city, Zion the abode of Thy glory, and Thy Temple. Rebuild

רוּךְ אַתָּה, יְיָ אֱלֹהֵינוּ,
מֶלֶךְ הָעוֹלָם, עַל הַגֶּפֶן
וְעַל פְּרִי הַגֶּפֶן, וְעַל
תְּנוּבַת הַשָּׂדֶה, וְעַל אֶרֶץ חֶמְדָּה
טוֹבָה וּרְחָבָה שֶׁרָצִיתָ וְהִנְחַלְתָּ
לַאֲבוֹתֵינוּ לֶאֱכֹל מִפִּרְיָהּ וְלִשְׂבֹּעַ
מִטּוּבָהּ. רַחֶם נָא, יְיָ אֱלֹהֵינוּ, עַל
יִשְׂרָאֵל עַמֶּךָ, וְעַל יְרוּשָׁלַיִם עִירֶךָ,
וְעַל צִיּוֹן מִשְׁכַּן כְּבוֹדֶךָ, וְעַל מִזְבְּחֲךָ

64

Jerusalem the holy city, speedily and in our lifetime. Lead us there and make us rejoice in its re-establishment, that we may eat of its fruit and enjoy its blessings so that we may praise Thee there in holiness and purity. [May it be Thy will to strengthen us on the Sabbath day.] Make us rejoice on this Festival of Unleavened Bread. For to Thee, O Lord, who art good and beneficent to all, we give thanks for that land and for the fruit of its vine. Praised be Thou, O Lord, for the land and for the fruit of the vine.

וְעַל הֵיכָלֶךָ. וּבְנֵה יְרוּשָׁלַיִם עִיר הַקֹּדֶשׁ בִּמְהֵרָה בְיָמֵינוּ, וְהַעֲלֵנוּ לְתוֹכָהּ וְשַׂמְּחֵנוּ בְּבִנְיָנָהּ, וְנֹאכַל מִפִּרְיָהּ וְנִשְׂבַּע מִטּוּבָהּ, וּנְבָרֶכְךָ עָלֶיהָ בִּקְדֻשָּׁה וּבְטָהֳרָה. [רְצֵה וְהַחֲלִיצֵנוּ בְּיוֹם הַשַּׁבָּת הַזֶּה, וְ]שַׂמְּחֵנוּ בְּיוֹם חַג הַמַּצּוֹת הַזֶּה. כִּי אַתָּה, יְיָ, טוֹב וּמֵטִיב לַכֹּל, וְנוֹדֶה לְּךָ עַל הָאָרֶץ וְעַל פְּרִי הַגָּפֶן. בָּרוּךְ אַתָּה, יְיָ, עַל הָאָרֶץ וְעַל פְּרִי הַגָּפֶן.

15. Nirtzah — <small>CONCLUDE THE SEDER.</small> —

The following verses are from the conclusion of a PIYYUT that enumerated all the regulations of the Seder.

Now is our Seder concluded,
Each custom and law fulfilled;
As we gathered to celebrate a
  Seder this night,
May we be worthy in freedom
  next year
Again to celebrate a Seder.

חֲסַל סִדּוּר פֶּסַח כְּהִלְכָתוֹ,
כְּכָל מִשְׁפָּטוֹ וְחֻקָּתוֹ;
כַּאֲשֶׁר זָכִינוּ לְסַדֵּר אוֹתוֹ,
כֵּן נִזְכֶּה לַעֲשׂוֹתוֹ.

O Pure One, who dwellest on high,
Raise up Thy numberless flock,
Speedily lead Thou the shoots of
  Thy stock
Redeemed, to Zion with song.

זָךְ שׁוֹכֵן מְעוֹנָה,
קוֹמֵם קְהַל עֲדַת מִי מָנָה;
בְּקָרוֹב נַהֵל נִטְעֵי כַנָּה,
פְּדוּיִם לְצִיּוֹן בְּרִנָּה.

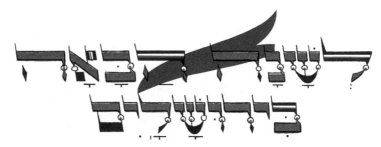

LE-SHANAH HA-BA-AH BI-Y'RUSHA-LA-YIM!
NEXT YEAR IN JERUSALEM!

Twice a year the traditional Jew exclaims: "Next year in Jerusalem!" — once at the Seder and again on the Day of Atonement after the Shofar is sounded at the conclusion of the NEILAH SERVICE. In their centuries of wandering, this affirmation, "Next year in Jerusalem!" encouraged the Jews to renew their faith in the restoration of Zion. At long last this is being realized in our day. "Freedom gave birth to Passover, and Passover gives birth to freedom." So writes a contemporary scholar.

IN GRATITUDE FOR THE CREATION OF THE STATE OF ISRAEL.

Fill an additional cup of wine.*

It has been explained that at the Seder we drink four cups of wine, symbolic of the four verses of redemption mentioned in the Bible. These are followed by a fifth verse, most appropriate in commemorating the dramatic events preceding the return of our people to Zion: וְהֵבֵאתִי v'HE-VE-TI, "And I will bring you in unto the land that I solemnly vowed to give to Abraham, to Isaac, and to Jacob; and I will give it to you for a heritage; I am the Lord." (Ex. 6:8)

Seven nations conspired to destroy the newly created State of Israel and push its inhabitants into the sea. But they were repulsed as was foretold: "The Lord will cause your enemies that rise up against you, to be routed before you; they shall come out against you one way, but they shall flee before you seven ways." (Deut. 28:7) What transpired in ERETZ YISRAEL is additional evidence to the believer, of the "Hand of God" in history, a modern miracle as impressive as any recorded in our Bible.

In gratitude for the creation of the State of Israel which we hope shall forever be established upon justice and truth, let us rise and drink another cup of wine.

בָּרוּךְ אַתָּה יְיָ אֱלֹהֵינוּ מֶלֶךְ הָעוֹלָם בּוֹרֵא פְּרִי הַגָּפֶן:

Baruḥ atta Adonai, elohenu meleḥ ha-olam, boray p'ri ha-gafen.
**Praised be Thou, O Lord our God, King of the Universe,
Creator of the Fruit of the Vine.**

הוֹדוּ לַיְיָ כִּי טוֹב כִּי לְעוֹלָם חַסְדּוֹ.

Give thanks unto the Lord for He is good;
His mercy is everlasting.

---

* The drinking of this additional cup of wine is optional.

66

For centuries, the declaration "Next year in Jerusalem!" marked the formal conclusion of the Seder. But, reluctant to leave the Seder table, later generations added new songs and new hymns. At first, these hymns were similar to the synagogue liturgy of Passover. Later, in order to hold the attention of the children, religious folksongs, madrigals of numbers, and nursery rhymes were included. When printing was introduced, these hymns became a standard part of the Haggadah. Parents and children, zestfully singing together, cherish through life these delightful melodies which, with the passing years, become increasingly dear to them.

כִּי לוֹ נָאֶה

KI LO NAEH

The following folk-poem in alphabetical acrostic, of unknown authorship, was probably composed in the Middle Ages in France or Germany. Some scholars ascribe it to Rabbi Eleazar Ha-Kalir of the eighth century. The Biblical phrases are from the following books: Psalms, Job, Deuteronomy, Jeremiah, Chronicles and Isaiah.

To God praise belongs;	כִּי לוֹ נָאֶה,
To Him it is ever due.	כִּי לוֹ יָאֶה.

Mighty in kingship,	אַ דִּיר בִּמְלוּכָה,
Chosen as of right;	בָּ חוּר כַּהֲלָכָה,
To Him His host of angels sing:	גְּ דוּדָיו יֹאמְרוּ לוֹ:
"To Thee, just to Thee,	לְךָ וּלְךָ,
To Thee and to Thee alone;	לְךָ כִּי לְךָ,
To Thee, yea, only to Thee,	לְךָ אַף לְךָ,
To Thee, O Lord, is sovereignty."	לְךָ יְיָ הַמַּמְלָכָה.
To God praise belongs;	כִּי לוֹ נָאֶה,
To Him it is ever due.	כִּי לוֹ יָאֶה.

Foremost in kingship,	דָּ גוּל בִּמְלוּכָה,
Glorious as of right;	הָ דוּר כַּהֲלָכָה,
To Him His faithful sing:	וָ תִיקָיו יֹאמְרוּ לוֹ:
"To Thee, just to Thee,	לְךָ וּלְךָ,
To Thee and to Thee alone;	לְךָ כִּי לְךָ,

To Thee, yea, only to Thee,	לְךָ אַף לְךָ,
To Thee, O Lord, is sovereignty."	לְךָ יְיָ הַמַּמְלָכָה.
To God praise belongs;	כִּי לוֹ נָאֶה,
To Him it is ever due.	כִּי לוֹ יָאֶה.
All-pure in kingship,	זַ כַּאי בִּמְלוּכָה,
Powerful as of right;	חָ סִין כַּהֲלָכָה,
To Him His courtiers sing:	טַ פְסְרָיו יֹאמְרוּ לוֹ:
"To Thee, just to Thee,	לְךָ וּלְךָ,
To Thee and to Thee alone;	לְךָ כִּי לְךָ,
To Thee, yea, only to Thee,	לְךָ אַף לְךָ,
To Thee, O Lord, is sovereignty."	לְךָ יְיָ הַמַּמְלָכָה.
To God praise belongs;	כִּי לוֹ נָאֶה,
To Him it is ever due.	כִּי לוֹ יָאֶה.
One alone in kingship,	יָ חִיד בִּמְלוּכָה,
Mighty as of right;	כַּ בִּיר כַּהֲלָכָה,
To Him His disciples sing:	לַ מּוּדָיו יֹאמְרוּ לוֹ:
"To Thee, just to Thee,	לְךָ וּלְךָ,
To Thee and to Thee alone;	לְךָ כִּי לְךָ,
To Thee, yea, only to Thee,	לְךָ אַף לְךָ,
To Thee, O Lord, is sovereignty."	לְךָ יְיָ הַמַּמְלָכָה.
To God praise belongs;	כִּי לוֹ נָאֶה,
To Him it is ever due.	כִּי לוֹ יָאֶה.
Exalted in kingship,	מַ וֹשֵׁל בִּמְלוּכָה,
Revered as of right;	נַ וֹרָא כַּהֲלָכָה,
To Him His angels sing:	סַ בִיבָיו יֹאמְרוּ לוֹ:
"To Thee, just to Thee,	לְךָ וּלְךָ,
To Thee and to Thee alone;	לְךָ כִּי לְךָ,
To Thee, yea, only to Thee,	לְךָ אַף לְךָ,
To Thee, O Lord, is sovereignty."	לְךָ יְיָ הַמַּמְלָכָה.

To God praise belongs;	כִּי לוֹ נָאֶה.
To Him it is ever due.	כִּי לוֹ יָאֶה.
Humble in kingship,	עָנָו בִּמְלוּכָה,
Redeeming as of right;	פּוֹדֶה כַּהֲלָכָה,
To Him the righteous sing:	צַדִּיקָיו יֹאמְרוּ לוֹ:
"To Thee, just to Thee,	לְךָ וּלְךָ,
To Thee and to Thee alone;	לְךָ כִּי לְךָ,
To Thee, yea, only to Thee,	לְךָ אַף לְךָ,
To Thee, O Lord, is sovereignty."	לְךָ יְיָ הַמַּמְלָכָה.
To God praise belongs;	כִּי לוֹ נָאֶה.
To Him it is ever due.	כִּי לוֹ יָאֶה.
Holy in kingship,	קָדוֹשׁ בִּמְלוּכָה,
Merciful as of right;	רַחוּם כַּהֲלָכָה,
To Him His myriad hosts sing:	שִׁנְאַנָּיו יֹאמְרוּ לוֹ:
"To Thee, just to Thee,	לְךָ וּלְךָ,
To Thee and to Thee alone;	לְךָ כִּי לְךָ,
To Thee, yea, only to Thee,	לְךָ אַף לְךָ,
To Thee, O Lord, is sovereignty."	לְךָ יְיָ הַמַּמְלָכָה.
To God praise belongs;	כִּי לוֹ נָאֶה,
To Him it is ever due.	כִּי לוֹ יָאֶה.
All-powerful in kingship,	תַּקִּיף בִּמְלוּכָה,
Sustaining as of right;	תּוֹמֵךְ כַּהֲלָכָה,
To Him the upright sing:	תְּמִימָיו יֹאמְרוּ לוֹ:
"To Thee, just to Thee,	לְךָ וּלְךָ,
To Thee and to Thee alone;	לְךָ כִּי לְךָ,
To Thee, yea, only to Thee,	לְךָ אַף לְךָ,
To Thee, O Lord, is sovereignty."	לְךָ יְיָ הַמַּמְלָכָה.
To God praise belongs;	כִּי לוֹ נָאֶה,
To Him it is ever due.	כִּי לוֹ יָאֶה.

אַדִּיר הוּא

ADDIR HU

The melody of the following poem, composed in alphabetical acrostic, has been popular for several centuries. The author is unknown. The theme is the speedy restoration of Zion, symbolized by the rebuilding of the Temple. It is metrically arranged so that it may be sung in English if desired.

Mighty is He! Mighty is He!	אַ דִּיר הוּא, אַדִּיר הוּא,
May He build His Temple soon.	יִבְנֶה בֵיתוֹ בְּקָרוֹב,
Speedily, speedily,	בִּמְהֵרָה בִּמְהֵרָה
In our lifetime may it be.	בְּיָמֵינוּ בְּקָרוֹב,
Build, O Lord! Build, O Lord!	אֵל בְּנֵה, אֵל בְּנֵה !
Build Thy Temple speedily!	בְּנֵה בֵיתְךָ בְּקָרוֹב !
Chosen, great, renowned is He!	בָּ חוּר הוּא, גָּ דוֹל הוּא, דָּ גוּל הוּא,
May He build His Temple soon.	יִבְנֶה בֵיתוֹ בְּקָרוֹב.
Speedily, speedily,	בִּמְהֵרָה בִּמְהֵרָה
In our lifetime may it be.	בְּיָמֵינוּ בְּקָרוֹב,
Build, O Lord! Build, O Lord!	אֵל בְּנֵה, אֵל בְּנֵה !
Build Thy Temple speedily!	בְּנֵה בֵיתְךָ בְּקָרוֹב !
Glorious, faithful, pure is He!	הָ דוּר הוּא, וָ תִיק הוּא, זַ כַּאי הוּא,
May He build His Temple soon.	יִבְנֶה בֵיתוֹ בְּקָרוֹב,
Speedily, speedily,	בִּמְהֵרָה בִּמְהֵרָה
In our lifetime may it be.	בְּיָמֵינוּ בְּקָרוֹב,
Build, O Lord! Build, O Lord!	אֵל בְּנֵה, אֵל בְּנֵה !
Build Thy Temple speedily!	בְּנֵה בֵיתְךָ בְּקָרוֹב !
Righteous, faultless, One is He!	חָ סִיד הוּא, טָ הוֹר הוּא, יָ חִיד הוּא,
May He build His Temple soon.	יִבְנֶה בֵיתוֹ בְּקָרוֹב,
Speedily, speedily,	בִּמְהֵרָה בִּמְהֵרָה
In our lifetime may it be.	בְּיָמֵינוּ בְּקָרוֹב,

Build, O Lord! Build, O Lord!

אֵל בְּנֵה, אֵל בְּנֵה!

Build Thy Temple speedily!

בְּנֵה בֵיתְךָ בְּקָרוֹב!

Mighty, wise and King is He!

כַּבִּיר הוּא, לָמוּד הוּא, מֶלֶךְ הוּא,

May He build His Temple soon.

יִבְנֶה בֵיתוֹ בְּקָרוֹב,

Speedily, speedily,

בִּמְהֵרָה בִּמְהֵרָה

In our lifetime may it be.

בְּיָמֵינוּ בְּקָרוֹב,

Build, O Lord! Build, O Lord!

אֵל בְּנֵה, אֵל בְּנֵה!

Build Thy Temple speedily!

בְּנֵה בֵיתְךָ בְּקָרוֹב!

Revered, exalted, strong is He!

נוֹרָא הוּא, סַגִּיב הוּא, עִזּוּז הוּא,

May He build His Temple soon.

יִבְנֶה בֵיתוֹ בְּקָרוֹב,

Speedily, speedily,

בִּמְהֵרָה בִּמְהֵרָה

In our lifetime may it be.

בְּיָמֵינוּ בְּקָרוֹב,

Build, O Lord! Build, O Lord!

אֵל בְּנֵה, אֵל בְּנֵה!

Build Thy Temple speedily!

בְּנֵה בֵיתְךָ בְּקָרוֹב!

Redeeming, holy, just is He!

פּוֹדֶה הוּא, צַדִּיק הוּא, קָדוֹשׁ הוּא,

May He build His Temple soon.

יִבְנֶה בֵיתוֹ בְּקָרוֹב,

Speedily, speedily,

בִּמְהֵרָה בִּמְהֵרָה

In our lifetime may it be.

בְּיָמֵינוּ בְּקָרוֹב,

Build, O Lord! Build, O Lord!

אֵל בְּנֵה, אֵל בְּנֵה!

Build Thy Temple speedily!

בְּנֵה בֵיתְךָ בְּקָרוֹב!

Almighty, merciful Lord is He!

רַחוּם הוּא, שַׁדַּי הוּא, תַּקִּיף הוּא,

May He build His Temple soon.

יִבְנֶה בֵיתוֹ בְּקָרוֹב,

Speedily, speedily,

בִּמְהֵרָה בִּמְהֵרָה

In our lifetime may it be.

בְּיָמֵינוּ בְּקָרוֹב,

Build, O Lord! Build, O Lord!

אֵל בְּנֵה, אֵל בְּנֵה!

Build Thy Temple speedily!

בְּנֵה בֵיתְךָ בְּקָרוֹב!

71

THE "NUMBER" MADRIGAL

In the following selection, we have an ancient forerunner of the modern quiz program. To hold the interest of the children, the host at the Seder asks questions pertaining to the history and beliefs of Judaism. The "number" madrigals invariably stopped at twelve, because thirteen was considered unlucky. But Judaism, frowning upon superstition, included the number thirteen. At thirteen, the boy becomes Bar Mitzvah. Thirteen are the creeds enumerated by Maimonides; thirteen are the attributes of God. Thirteen is the numerical value of the Hebrew letters in the word EHAD, which means "ONE," and refers to the unity of God, which is stressed throughout this selection.

The Leader asks the questions and the participants answer.

Who knows the answer to one?	אֶחָד מִי יוֹדֵעַ?
I know the answer to one. ONE is our God, In heaven and on earth.	אֶחָד אֲנִי יוֹדֵעַ: אֶחָד אֱלֹהֵינוּ שֶׁבַּשָּׁמַיִם וּבָאָרֶץ.
Who knows the answer to two?	שְׁנַיִם מִי יוֹדֵעַ?
I know the answer to two. TWO are Sinai's tablets.	שְׁנַיִם אֲנִי יוֹדֵעַ: שְׁנֵי לֻחוֹת הַבְּרִית,
But One alone is our God, In heaven and on earth.	אֶחָד אֱלֹהֵינוּ שֶׁבַּשָּׁמַיִם וּבָאָרֶץ.
Who knows the answer to three?	שְׁלֹשָׁה מִי יוֹדֵעַ?
I know the answer to three. THREE are the patriarch fathers; Two are Sinai's tablets.	שְׁלֹשָׁה אֲנִי יוֹדֵעַ: שְׁלֹשָׁה אָבוֹת, שְׁנֵי לֻחוֹת הַבְּרִית,
But One alone is our God, In heaven and on earth.	אֶחָד אֱלֹהֵינוּ שֶׁבַּשָּׁמַיִם וּבָאָרֶץ.
Who knows the answer to four?	אַרְבַּע מִי יוֹדֵעַ?
I know the answer to four. FOUR are the mothers of Israel; Three are the patriarch fathers; Two are Sinai's tablets.	אַרְבַּע אֲנִי יוֹדֵעַ: אַרְבַּע אִמָּהוֹת, שְׁלֹשָׁה אָבוֹת, שְׁנֵי לֻחוֹת הַבְּרִית,

72

But One alone is our God,
In heaven and on earth.

אֶחָד אֱלֹהֵינוּ
שֶׁבַּשָּׁמַיִם וּבָאָרֶץ.

Who knows the answer
to five?

חֲמִשָּׁה מִי יוֹדֵעַ?

I know the answer to five.
FIVE are the Books of Moses;
Four are the mothers of Israel;
Three are the patriarch fathers;
Two are Sinai's tablets.

חֲמִשָּׁה אֲנִי יוֹדֵעַ:
חֲמִשָּׁה חֻמְשֵׁי תוֹרָה,
אַרְבַּע אִמָּהוֹת,
שְׁלֹשָׁה אָבוֹת,
שְׁנֵי לֻחוֹת הַבְּרִית,

But One alone is our God,
In heaven and on earth.

אֶחָד אֱלֹהֵינוּ
שֶׁבַּשָּׁמַיִם וּבָאָרֶץ.

Who knows the answer
to six?

שִׁשָּׁה מִי יוֹדֵעַ?

I know the answer to six.
SIX are the volumes of Mishnah;
Five are the Books of Moses;
Four are the mothers of Israel;
Three are the patriarch fathers;
Two are Sinai's tablets.

שִׁשָּׁה אֲנִי יוֹדֵעַ:
שִׁשָּׁה סִדְרֵי מִשְׁנָה,
חֲמִשָּׁה חֻמְשֵׁי תוֹרָה,
אַרְבַּע אִמָּהוֹת,
שְׁלֹשָׁה אָבוֹת,
שְׁנֵי לֻחוֹת הַבְּרִית,

But One alone is our God,
In heaven and on earth.

אֶחָד אֱלֹהֵינוּ
שֶׁבַּשָּׁמַיִם וּבָאָרֶץ.

Who knows the answer
to seven?

שִׁבְעָה מִי יוֹדֵעַ?

I know the answer to seven.
SEVEN are the days of the week;
Six are the volumes of Mishnah;
Five are the Books of Moses;
Four are the mothers of Israel;
Three are the patriarch fathers;
Two are Sinai's tablets.

שִׁבְעָה אֲנִי יוֹדֵעַ:
שִׁבְעָה יְמֵי שַׁבַּתָּא,
שִׁשָּׁה סִדְרֵי מִשְׁנָה,
חֲמִשָּׁה חֻמְשֵׁי תוֹרָה,
אַרְבַּע אִמָּהוֹת,
שְׁלֹשָׁה אָבוֹת,
שְׁנֵי לֻחוֹת הַבְּרִית,

73

But One alone is our God,
In heaven and on earth.

אֶחָד אֱלֹהֵינוּ
שֶׁבַּשָּׁמַיִם וּבָאָרֶץ.

Who knows the answer
to eight?

שְׁמֹנָה מִי יוֹדֵעַ?

I know the answer to eight.
EIGHT are the days to the
covenant;
Seven are the days of the week;
Six are the volumes of Mishnah;
Five are the Books of Moses;
Four are the mothers of Israel;
Three are the patriarch fathers;
Two are Sinai's tablets.

שְׁמֹנָה אֲנִי יוֹדֵעַ:
שְׁמֹנָה יְמֵי מִילָה,
שִׁבְעָה יְמֵי שַׁבַּתָּא,
שִׁשָּׁה סִדְרֵי מִשְׁנָה,
חֲמִשָּׁה חֻמְשֵׁי תוֹרָה,
אַרְבַּע אִמָּהוֹת,
שְׁלֹשָׁה אָבוֹת,
שְׁנֵי לֻחוֹת הַבְּרִית,

But One alone is our God,
In heaven and on earth.

אֶחָד אֱלֹהֵינוּ
שֶׁבַּשָּׁמַיִם וּבָאָרֶץ.

Who knows the answer
to nine?

תִּשְׁעָה מִי יוֹדֵעַ?

I know the answer to nine.
NINE are the months to child-
birth;
Eight are the days to the
covenant;
Seven are the days of the week;
Six are the volumes of Mishnah;
Five are the Books of Moses;
Four are the mothers of Israel;
Three are the patriarch fathers;
Two are Sinai's tablets.

תִּשְׁעָה אֲנִי יוֹדֵעַ:
תִּשְׁעָה יַרְחֵי לֵדָה,
שְׁמֹנָה יְמֵי מִילָה,
שִׁבְעָה יְמֵי שַׁבַּתָּא,
שִׁשָּׁה סִדְרֵי מִשְׁנָה,
חֲמִשָּׁה חֻמְשֵׁי תוֹרָה,
אַרְבַּע אִמָּהוֹת,
שְׁלֹשָׁה אָבוֹת,
שְׁנֵי לֻחוֹת הַבְּרִית,

But One alone is our God,
In heaven and on earth.

אֶחָד אֱלֹהֵינוּ
שֶׁבַּשָּׁמַיִם וּבָאָרֶץ.

עֲשָׂרָה מִי יוֹדֵעַ?

עֲשָׂרָה אֲנִי יוֹדֵעַ:
עֲשָׂרָה דִבְּרַיָּא,
תִּשְׁעָה יַרְחֵי לֵדָה,
שְׁמֹנָה יְמֵי מִילָה,
שִׁבְעָה יְמֵי שַׁבַּתָּא,
שִׁשָּׁה סִדְרֵי מִשְׁנָה,
חֲמִשָּׁה חֻמְשֵׁי תוֹרָה,
אַרְבַּע אִמָּהוֹת,
שְׁלֹשָׁה אָבוֹת,
שְׁנֵי לֻחוֹת הַבְּרִית,
אֶחָד אֱלֹהֵינוּ
שֶׁבַּשָּׁמַיִם וּבָאָרֶץ.

אַחַד עָשָׂר מִי יוֹדֵעַ?

אַחַד עָשָׂר אֲנִי יוֹדֵעַ:
אַחַד עָשָׂר כּוֹכְבַיָּא,
עֲשָׂרָה דִבְּרַיָּא,
תִּשְׁעָה יַרְחֵי לֵדָה,
שְׁמֹנָה יְמֵי מִילָה,
שִׁבְעָה יְמֵי שַׁבַּתָּא,
שִׁשָּׁה סִדְרֵי מִשְׁנָה,
חֲמִשָּׁה חֻמְשֵׁי תוֹרָה,
אַרְבַּע אִמָּהוֹת,
שְׁלֹשָׁה אָבוֹת,
שְׁנֵי לֻחוֹת הַבְּרִית,
אֶחָד אֱלֹהֵינוּ
שֶׁבַּשָּׁמַיִם וּבָאָרֶץ.

Who knows the answer to ten?

I know the answer to ten.
TEN are the divine commandments;
Nine are the months to childbirth;
Eight are the days to the covenant;
Seven are the days of the week;
Six are the volumes of Mishnah;
Five are the Books of Moses;
Four are the mothers of Israel;
Three are the patriarch fathers;
Two are Sinai's tablets.

But One alone is our God,
In heaven and on earth.

Who knows the answer to eleven?

I know the answer to eleven.
ELEVEN are the stars in Joseph's dream;
Ten are the divine commandments;
Nine are the months to childbirth;
Eight are the days to the covenant;
Seven are the days of the week;
Six are the volumes of Mishnah;
Five are the Books of Moses;
Four are the mothers of Israel;
Three are the patriarch fathers;
Two are Sinai's tablets.

But One alone is our God,
In heaven and on earth.

Who knows the answer to twelve?

I know the answer to twelve.
TWELVE are the tribes of Israel;
Eleven are the stars in Joseph's dream;
Ten are the divine commandments;
Nine are the months to childbirth;
Eight are the days to the covenant;
Seven are the days of the week;
Six are the volumes of Mishnah;
Five are the Books of Moses;
Four are the mothers of Israel;
Three are the patriarch fathers;
Two are Sinai's tablets.

But One alone is our God,
In heaven and on earth.

Who knows the answer to thirteen?

I know the answer to thirteen.
THIRTEEN are the attributes of God;*
Twelve are the tribes of Israel;
Eleven are the stars in Joseph's dream;
Ten are the divine commandments;
Nine are the months to childbirth;
Eight are the days to the covenant;
Seven are the days of the week;
Six are the volumes of Mishnah;
Five are the Books of Moses;
Four are the mothers of Israel;
Three are the patriarch fathers;
Two are Sinai's tablets.

But One alone is our God,
In heaven and on earth.

שְׁנֵים עָשָׂר מִי יוֹדֵעַ?

שְׁנֵים עָשָׂר אֲנִי יוֹדֵעַ:
שְׁנֵים עָשָׂר שִׁבְטַיָּא,
אַחַד עָשָׂר כּוֹכְבַיָּא,
עֲשָׂרָה דִבְּרַיָּא,
תִּשְׁעָה יַרְחֵי לֵדָה,
שְׁמֹנָה יְמֵי מִילָה,
שִׁבְעָה יְמֵי שַׁבַּתָּא,
שִׁשָּׁה סִדְרֵי מִשְׁנָה,
חֲמִשָּׁה חֻמְשֵׁי תוֹרָה,
אַרְבַּע אִמָּהוֹת,
שְׁלֹשָׁה אָבוֹת,
שְׁנֵי לֻחוֹת הַבְּרִית,
אֶחָד אֱלֹהֵינוּ
שֶׁבַּשָּׁמַיִם וּבָאָרֶץ.

שְׁלֹשָׁה עָשָׂר מִי יוֹדֵעַ?

שְׁלֹשָׁה עָשָׂר אֲנִי יוֹדֵעַ:
שְׁלֹשָׁה עָשָׂר מִדַּיָּא,
שְׁנֵים עָשָׂר שִׁבְטַיָּא,
אַחַד עָשָׂר כּוֹכְבַיָּא,
עֲשָׂרָה דִבְּרַיָּא,
תִּשְׁעָה יַרְחֵי לֵדָה,
שְׁמֹנָה יְמֵי מִילָה,
שִׁבְעָה יְמֵי שַׁבַּתָּא,
שִׁשָּׁה סִדְרֵי מִשְׁנָה,
חֲמִשָּׁה חֻמְשֵׁי תוֹרָה,
אַרְבַּע אִמָּהוֹת,
שְׁלֹשָׁה אָבוֹת,
שְׁנֵי לֻחוֹת הַבְּרִית,
אֶחָד אֱלֹהֵינוּ
שֶׁבַּשָּׁמַיִם וּבָאָרֶץ.

---

* Exodus 34: 6, 7.

76

חַד גַּדְיָא

ḤAD GADYA

Written in Aramaic, thus pointing to its ancient origin, ḤAD GADYA did not become part of the Haggadah until it was included in the Prague edition of 1590. Though ḤAD GADYA is similar in style to the folk tales of the Middle Ages, and to such nursery rhymes as "The House that Jack Built," it differs from them in that it teaches a moral lesson. Because the Seder is child-centered and geared to keep the children alert to the very end, ḤAD GADYA may have originally been designed to hold their interest, but noted scholars read significant truths into this song. It voices the concept of divine justice. It intimates that there is retribution in store for all oppressors and that, in the scheme of society and government, everyone is responsible to someone higher, with God supreme above all.

Rabbi Jonathan Eybeschütz and others have interpreted ḤAD GADYA as a hymn to God's providence. God is evident in the history of mankind. Israel (The Kid), redeemed by God from Egypt through Moses and Aaron (the two zuzim), succumbs to a mightier empire which, in turn, is defeated by other empires, etc., until God's rule of justice triumphs. The cat is Assyria; the dog, Babylonia; the stick, Persia; the water, Greece; the ox, Rome; the slaughterer, the Moslems; the angel of death, the European nations. The Holy One will finally suppress all tyranny, deliver all His children from oppression, re-establish the principle of justice, and bring about the era of peace for all nations. The Seder thus ends on a hopeful and joyous note. Through the Seder we keep alive humanity's love for freedom.

ḤAD GADYA

An only kid! An only kid!	חַד גַּדְיָא, חַד גַּדְיָא,
My father bought for two zuzim.	דְּזַבִּן אַבָּא בִּתְרֵי זוּזֵי;
An only kid! An only kid!	חַד גַּדְיָא, חַד גַּדְיָא !

Then came a cat	וְאָתָא שׁוּנְרָא
And ate the kid,	וְאָכַל לְגַדְיָא,
My father bought for two zuzim.	דְּזַבִּן אַבָּא בִּתְרֵי זוּזֵי;
An only kid! An only kid!	חַד גַּדְיָא, חַד גַּדְיָא !

Then came a dog	וְאָתָא כַלְבָּא
And bit the cat,	וְנָשַׁךְ לְשׁוּנְרָא,
That ate the kid,	דְּאָכַל לְגַדְיָא,
My father bought for two zuzim.	דְּזַבִּן אַבָּא בִּתְרֵי זוּזֵי;
An only kid! An only kid!	חַד גַּדְיָא, חַד גַּדְיָא !

Then came a stick	וְאָתָא חוּטְרָא
And beat the dog,	וְהִכָּה לְכַלְבָּא,
That bit the cat,	דְּנָשַׁךְ לְשׁוּנְרָא,
That ate the kid,	דְּאָכַל לְגַדְיָא,
My father bought for two zuzim.	דְּזַבִּן אַבָּא בִּתְרֵי זוּזֵי;
An only kid! An only kid!	חַד גַּדְיָא, חַד גַּדְיָא !

Then came a fire	וְאָתָא נוּרָא
And burned the stick,	וְשָׂרַף לְחוּטְרָא,
That beat the dog,	דְּהִכָּה לְכַלְבָּא,
That bit the cat,	דְּנָשַׁךְ לְשׁוּנְרָא,
That ate the kid,	דְּאָכַל לְגַדְיָא,
My father bought for two zuzim.	דְּזַבִּן אַבָּא בִּתְרֵי זוּזֵי;
An only kid! An only kid!	חַד גַּדְיָא, חַד גַּדְיָא !

Then came water	וְאָתָא מַיָּא
And quenched the fire	וְכָבָה לְנוּרָא,
That burned the stick	דְּשָׂרַף לְחוּטְרָא,
That beat the dog	דְּהִכָּה לְכַלְבָּא,
That bit the cat	דְּנָשַׁךְ לְשׁוּנְרָא,
That ate the kid	דְּאָכַל לְגַדְיָא,
My father bought for two zuzim.	דְּזַבִּן אַבָּא בִּתְרֵי זוּזֵי;
An only kid! An only kid!	חַד גַּדְיָא, חַד גַּדְיָא !

Then came an ox	וְאָתָא תוֹרָא
And drank the water	וְשָׁתָה לְמַיָּא,
That quenched the fire	דְּכָבָה לְנוּרָא,
That burned the stick	דְּשָׂרַף לְחוּטְרָא,
That beat the dog	דְּהִכָּה לְכַלְבָּא,
That bit the cat	דְּנָשַׁךְ לְשׁוּנְרָא,
That ate the kid	דְּאָכַל לְגַדְיָא,
My father bought for two zuzim.	דְּזַבִּן אַבָּא בִּתְרֵי זוּזֵי;
An only kid! An only kid!	חַד גַּדְיָא, חַד גַּדְיָא !

Then came a slaughterer	וְאָתָא הַשּׁוֹחֵט
And killed the ox	וְשָׁחַט לְתוֹרָא,
That drank the water	דְּשָׁתָה לְמַיָּא,
That quenched the fire	דְּכָבָה לְנוּרָא,
That burned the stick	דְּשָׂרַף לְחוּטְרָא,
That beat the dog	דְּהִכָּה לְכַלְבָּא,
That bit the cat	דְּנָשַׁךְ לְשׁוּנְרָא,
That ate the kid	דְּאָכַל לְגַדְיָא,
My father bought for two zuzim.	דְּזַבִּן אַבָּא בִּתְרֵי זוּזֵי;
An only kid! An only kid!	חַד גַּדְיָא, חַד גַּדְיָא !

Then came the angel of death	וְאָתָא מַלְאַךְ הַמָּוֶת,
And slew the slaughterer	וְשָׁחַט לַשּׁוֹחֵט,
Who killed the ox	דְּשָׁחַט לְתוֹרָא,
That drank the water	דְּשָׁתָה לְמַיָּא,
That quenched the fire	דְּכָבָה לְנוּרָא,
That burned the stick	דְּשָׂרַף לְחוּטְרָא,
That beat the dog	דְּהִכָּה לְכַלְבָּא,
That bit the cat	דְּנָשַׁךְ לְשׁוּנְרָא,
That ate the kid	דְּאָכַל לְגַדְיָא,
My father bought for two zuzim.	דְּזַבִּן אַבָּא בִּתְרֵי זוּזֵי;

An only kid! An only kid!   חַד גַּדְיָא, חַד גַּדְיָא !

Then came the Holy One, praised be He,	וְאָתָא הַקָּדוֹשׁ בָּרוּךְ הוּא,
And smote the angel of death	וְשָׁחַט לְמַלְאַךְ הַמָּוֶת,
Who slew the slaughterer	דְּשָׁחַט לַשּׁוֹחֵט,
Who killed the ox	דְּשָׁחַט לְתוֹרָא,
That drank the water	דְּשָׁתָה לְמַיָּא,
That quenched the fire	דְּכָבָה לְנוּרָא,
That burned the stick	דְּשָׂרַף לְחוּטְרָא,
That beat the dog	דְּהִכָּה לְכַלְבָּא,
That bit the cat	דְּנָשַׁךְ לְשׁוּנְרָא,
That ate the kid	דְּאָכַל לְגַדְיָא,
My father bought for two zuzim.	דְּזַבִּן אַבָּא בִּתְרֵי זוּזֵי;

An only kid! An only kid!   חַד גַּדְיָא, חַד גַּדְיָא !

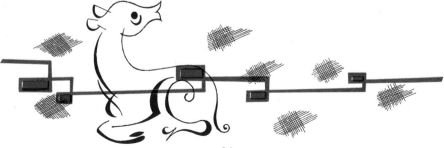

"Proclaim Liberty Throughout the Land, Unto All the Inhabitants Thereof." (Lev. 25:10)

In the Talmud, this verse is the subject of some lively discussion. One Sage asked: "Are we to proclaim liberty, as the verse implies, only in the Holy Land?" "No!" was the answer. "The law requires us to proclaim liberty everywhere, in all the countries of the world."

Liberty is indeed universal and indivisible. The world today has become a small neighborhood. As long as slavery exists anywhere, liberty is everywhere endangered. There cannot be permanent liberty in one country if there be tyranny in another. The new space age, with the possibility of nations claiming control of the planets, makes it imperative for mankind to proclaim liberty everywhere.

"If liberty is to be proclaimed everywhere," asked another of the Hebrew Sages, "why doesn't the verse specifically state, 'Proclaim liberty throughout the world?' Why does the verse say, 'Proclaim liberty throughout the land?'"

The answer is most illuminating. We must first proclaim liberty in the land in which we live, and make it a reality in our own country. It is easy to criticize other nations for discrimination because of race, color, or creed. We are required first to put our own house in order, and to remove injustice in our own land, so that our advocacy of liberty for all people shall have the ring of sincerity. As long as liberty shall truly exist in any one country, there is hope that it will spread throughout the world.

Like charity, liberty must begin at home. Freedom is not a static condition. It is a continuing, democratic process — a dynamic force dedicated to a sublime purpose. That purpose is to translate into life those words inscribed in the Declaration of Independence, which have their roots in the Bible:

"ALL MEN ... ARE ENDOWED BY THEIR CREATOR WITH CERTAIN INALIENABLE RIGHTS, THAT AMONG THESE ARE LIFE, LIBERTY AND THE PURSUIT OF HAPPINESS."

CLOSING PRAYER

Our God and God of our fathers, as we bring to a close this Seder, commemorating the exodus of our people from Egyptian bondage, we pray that we may carry with us into daily life the message of freedom emphasized in its symbols and rituals. May the memories of this night inspire us to cast off our own shackles of intolerance, greed and hatred. May we here resolve to break the chains that fetter our minds and blind us to the glory, beauty and goodness which life offers in such abundance.

Help us to realize that we cannot have freedom for ourselves unless we are willing to give it to others. Through our daily deeds and devotion, may each of us in our own way, help to liberate all who live in fear, poverty and oppression. May the light of freedom penetrate into all corners of the world, and lift the darkness of tyranny until tyranny is no more, so that all men may be free. Amen.

America

(4th Verse)

Our fathers' God, to Thee
Author of liberty,
To Thee we sing;
Long may our land be bright,
With freedom's holy light,
Protect us by Thy might,
Great God, our King!

התקוה

כָּל עוֹד בַּלֵּבָב פְּנִימָה. נֶפֶשׁ יְהוּדִי הוֹמִיָּה.
וּלְפַאֲתֵי מִזְרָח קָדִימָה. עַיִן לְצִיּוֹן צוֹפִיָּה:
עוֹד לֹא אָבְדָה תִקְוָתֵנוּ. הַתִּקְוָה שְׁנוֹת אַלְפַּיִם.
לִהְיוֹת עַם חָפְשִׁי בְּאַרְצֵנוּ. בְּאֶרֶץ צִיּוֹן וִירוּשָׁלָיִם:

Kol od ba-ley-vav p'ni-ma
Nefesh y'hudi ho-miya.
U-l'fa-atay mizraḥ Kadima
Ayin l'tzion tzofiya.
Od lo avda tikva-tenu
Hatikva sh'not alpayim
Li-yot am ḥaf-shi b'artzay-nu
B'eretz tzion viy-ru-shalayim

PASSOVER SONGS

A-DEER HU (Page 70)

A-deer hu a-deer hu,
Yiv-neh vey-to b'ka-rov.

    Bim-hey-rah, bim-hey-rah,
    B'ya-mey-nu b'ka-rov.

    El b'ney, El b'ney
    B'ney veyt-ḥa b'ka-rov.

Ba-ḥur hu, ga-dol hu.
Da-gul hu, yiv-neh
Vey-to b'ka-rov.

    Bim-hey-rah . . .

Ha-dur hu va-tik hu, za-kay hu.
Yiv-hen vey-to b'ka-rov.

    Bim-hey-rah . . .

Ḥa-sid hu, ta-hor hu. Ya-ḥid hu,
Yiv-neh vey-to b'ka-rov.

    Bim-hey-rah . . .

E-HAD MEE YO-DAY-A? (Page 72)

E-ḥad mee yo-deya?
E-ḥad anee yo-dey-a.
E-ḥad Elohey-nu
She-be-sha-ma-yeem u-va-a-retz.

Sh'nayeem mee yo-dey-a?
Sh'nayeem anee yo-day-a.
Sh'ney lu-ḥot ha-b'rit,
E-ḥad Elo-hey-nu
She-ba-sha-ma-yeem u-va-a-retz.

Sh'lo-sha mee yo-day-a?
Sh'lo-sha anee yo-dey-a.
Sh'lo-sha a-vot,
Sh'ney lu-ḥot ha-b'rit,
E-ḥad Elo-hey-nu
She-ba-sha-ma-yeem u-va-a-retz.

Ar-ba mee yo-dey-a?
Ar-ba anee yo-dey-a.
Ar-ba ee-ma-hot,
Sh'lo-sha a-vot,
Sh'ney lu-ḥot ha-b'rit,
Eḥad Elo-hey-nu
She-ba-sha-ma-yeem u-va a-retz.

ḤAD GAD-YA (Page 79)

Ḥad gad-ya, ḥad gad-ya.

    Di-ze-van a-ba bit-rey zu-zey
    Ḥad gad-ya, ḥad gad-ya

V'ata shun-ra v'aḥal l'gad-ya.

        Di-ze-van . . .

V'ato ḥal-ba v'na-shaḥ l'shun-ra
D'a-ḥal l'gad-ya.

        Di-ze-van . . .

V'a-ta ḥut-ra v'hi-kah
   l'ḥal-ba
D'na-shaḥ l'shun-ra.
   D'a-ḥal l'gad-ya.

        Di-ze-van . . .

V'a-ta nu-ra v'sa-raf
   l'ḥut-ra
D'hi-kal l'ḥal-ba, d'na-shaḥ
   l'shun-ra,
D'a-ḥal l'gad-ya.

        Di-ze-van . . .

V'a-ta ma-ya v'ḥa-vah l'nu-ra
D'sa-raf l'ḥut-ra, d'hi-kah l'ḥal-ba,
D'na-shaḥ l'shun-ra,
D'a-ḥal l'gad-ya.

        Di-ze-van . . .